EXCAVATING
FORT RALEIGH

EXCAVATING
FORT RALEIGH

ARCHAEOLOGY AT ENGLAND'S FIRST COLONY

IVOR NOËL HUME

Edited by Dr. Eric Klingelhofer and Nicholas Luccketti

THE
History
PRESS

Published by The History Press
Charleston, SC
www.historypress.com

Presented by First Colony Foundation for NPS Fort Raleigh National Historic Site.

ISBN 9781467156448

Library of Congress Control Number: 2023948667

Project director Ivor Noël Hume and former NPS archaeologist J.C. Harrington at Fort Raleigh, 1991. *FCF.*

Site plan accompanying
First and Lost: In Search of America's First English Settlement
by Ivor Noël Hume

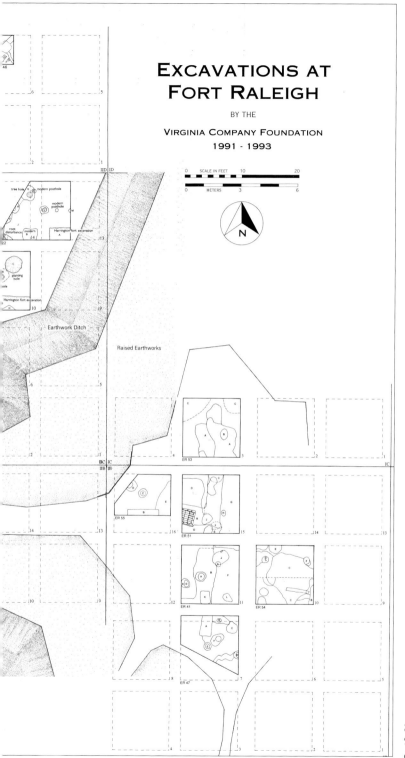

EXCAVATIONS AT
FORT RALEIGH

BY THE

VIRGINIA COMPANY FOUNDATION
1991 - 1993

0 SCALE IN FEET 10 20

0 METERS 3 6

N

tree hole   modern posthole

modern
posthole

root
disturbance   modern

Harrington fort excavation

planting
hole

Harrington fort excavation

Earthwork Ditch

Raised Earthworks

ER 53

ER 55

ER 51

ER 41

ER 54

ER 47

Site plan of 1991–
92 excavations. *Plan
drawn by JM.*

For
Jean Carl "Pinky" Harrington
and
Virginia S. Harrington,

who together carried the lamp
long before many of us could see the light.

CONTENTS

Illustrations   13
Author's Preface   15
Editors' Preface   19
Foreword, by David E. Hallac, National Park Service   21
Foreword, by Phillip W. Evans, First Colony Foundation   23
Introduction: In Search of America's First English Settlement   25

1. Amadas to White: A Historical Summary   27
2. Fort Raleigh: The Later History   54
3. Fort Raleigh: The Archaeology, 1947–85   73
4. More Archaeology, 1991–93   94
   Phase 1: The Preview   96
   Phase 2: The Search Expanded   98
   Phase 3: The 1992–93 Seasons   108
5. Things They Brought, Left or Took Away   124
6. The Fort Raleigh Earthwork: Evidence and Interpretations   149
7. The Future of the Past   154

Appendices   159
Notes   161
Select Bibliography   183
About the Author   189
About the Editors   191

ILLUSTRATIONS

When not attributed to an external source, illustrations were made by project director Ivor Noël Hume (INH), by archaeological draftsperson Jamie May (JM) or by other members of the excavation project.

AUTHOR'S PREFACE

Being painfully aware that most archaeological reports are incredibly dull and rarely read by anyone but professional reviewers, I asked the Fort Raleigh National Historic Site's mentor, Superintendent Thomas L. Hartman, what kind of report he would prefer: unreadable but every *t* crossed or relatively easy reading and cutting to the chase. He answered that he preferred the latter—which, because the national parks cater to a broad-based public, makes some sense. Anyone who cares deeply whether a potsherd from layer E.R.31D in area ill.D.15 was found in, over or under a layer of brown, sandy loam E.R.31C in area m.D.14 is free to consult the field records.

There are occasions, however, when such relationships are crucial to developing or assailing a theory, and in such instances, the dull details will be found either in the notes or appendices. For the most part, however, the archaeological discoveries act as metaphors, a flashlight to illuminate information already part of the Roanoke Island history. When they do so, they are discussed at possibly tiresome length, but when they don't, they are omitted.

Knowing that post mold A is two inches smaller than post mold B can be of paramount importance to a park designer planning to reconstruct the building whose roof those posts supported, but to a distant reader who has no intention of reconstructing anything, such information is worthless. What did they find, and how did it help advance the story of the Roanoke settlements? Those are the questions that draw visitors to the site and that may prompt others to plow through these pages. It is to the lay reader, therefore, that this study is addressed. There is, however, a second audience, no doubt much smaller, but in its way no less important: namely, curators, archaeologists and cultural historians elsewhere who find or are studying comparable science-related ceramics and glassware. For them, the assurance that the Fort Raleigh artifacts were deposited between September 1585 and June 1586 provides a unique dating window as narrow as an arrow slot. For this reason, therefore, the section on the artifacts is more discursive than would otherwise be necessary.

Those historians who, often with good reason, question the reliability of archaeological evidence also argue that archaeologists have no business playing with their toys—the written records of history. But a hands-off-history requirement on the part of archaeologists would propel them into the darkness of prehistory. To be of service to the past, it is imperative that the archaeologist makes use of all available evidence, be it physical or documentary. In these pages, therefore, the attempt is to better understand who did what, why and when on Roanoke Island between 1585 and 1590, and to that end, every artifact and every word has to be considered part of the puzzle. In short, this is as much a reexamination of the history as it is an account of what has been found in the ground.

Without the encouragement of Superintendent Hartman and his educational and management assistants Bebe Woody, Mary Moran, Charles Snow and historian Allen Smigielski, the 1991–93 fieldwork would not have been possible, nor would it have been permitted without the endorsement of the National Park Service's Southeast Regional archaeologist, Dr. Richard Faust. Indeed, it was thanks, also, to the pioneering work of Jean C. (Pinky) Harrington and his successor Dr. John E. Ehrenhard that the reinvestigation owed its being. It is impossible to overestimate the importance of the counsel provided by Fort Raleigh's longtime but unofficial historian Phillip Evans, who was unstinting in his readiness not only to debate and, where necessary, to disagree but also, in 1991, to dig. His discovery in 1982 of two wood-lined well shafts may be the most important clue to the location of the 1585–88 village that will ever be found. Valuable, too, was the advice and knowledge no less freely given by Wynn Dough, director of the Outer Banks History Center at Manteo.

In days of yore—so yore as to be barely remembered—archaeology was a vocational pursuit of anyone with an enquiring mind and a sharp spade. Today, it hews to professional standards and costs large sums of money, money that becomes increasingly hard to corral. Without two to-be-matched grants from the National Geographic Society, the Roanoke Project would not have moved further than the drawing board. Instead, with that support secured, several foundations, societies and individuals rallied to the cause.

The Virginia Company Foundation, which conducted the 1991–93 dig, is grateful, therefore, to the Kenan Foundation; the Elizabeth Hooper Foundation; Mr. Lawrence Lewis of Richmond, Virginia; Mr. James E. Maloney of Williamsburg; the late Miss Roberta C. Schumann of King City, Oregon; Mrs. R.S. Dean Sr. of Fort Myers, Florida; Dr. Thomas L. Munzel of Williamsburg; Mr. and Mrs. Thomas W. Wood, also of Williamsburg; and Mr. Robert B. Eggleston of Harrisonburg, Virginia. Special gratitude is extended to Mrs. G.B. Daversa, Mrs. G. Humphrey Bryan Jr. and Mrs. James E. Crews and her daughters, and to the National Society of Daughters of Founders and Patriots of America, not only for financial support but also for their keen interest in the progress of the work. Without their funds and their help in raising funds from others, the latest chapter on the Fort Raleigh story would almost certainly have remained unwritten.

For scientific analyses of the metallic evidence, First Colony Foundation is indebted to Dr. Robert M. Ehrenreich of the National Research Council, Dr. Peter Glumac of Engineering Science and Dr. Eric Eisenbraun and Dr. Alain Kaloyeros of the State University of New York at Albany; to Dr. W. Robert Kelly and his colleagues at the United States National Institute of Standards and Technology, as well as to Dr. R. Werner Soukup of Perchtoldsdorf, Austria. For the identification of wood samples, we are indebted to Dr. Dosia Laendecker at the Department of Anthropology, National Museum of Natural History, Smithsonian Institution. For drawing our attention to potential parallels found in excavations at the Tower of London, we are grateful to Mr. Geoffrey Parnell. Dr. Robert L. Davidson at the Carnegie Museum of Natural History and Dr. Frances B. King at the Center for Cultural Resource Research at the University of Pittsburgh commented on the botanical remains, and Dr. Gerald K. Kelso of the National Park Service helpfully offered advice regarding pollen analysis—alas, a resource unavailable due to ground contamination.

Money and expertise are essential contributions to any archaeological project, but none can succeed without the dedication and labor of the people who do the digging. Leading the team for the Virginia Company Foundation were Dr. William Kelso, then of the Thomas Jefferson Memorial Foundation, and Mr. Nicholas Luccketti from James River Institute for Archaeology; Dr. Eric Klingelhofer from Mercer University; and Dr. Carter Hudgins from Mary Washington College. They were supported by Messrs.

David Hazzard, Nathaniel Smith, William Leigh, Alastair Macdonald, Dr. James Barton and Mesdames Martha Williams, Jamie May and the late curator Audrey Noël Hume. Representing the National Park Service was Dr. Bennie C. Keel, archaeologist for its Southeastern Archeological Center, in 1992 aided by E. Cornelison, D. Leslie and S. Walker. In addition, the Roanoke Project was most diligently and ably supported by six local people who knew nothing about archaeology when they joined the crew as dirt movers (whom we called servitors) but who became invaluable contributors before they were through: Susanne Wrenn, Alice Snow, Ward Hall, Brian Kersey, Stephen Ryan and Michael Gery.

Finally, I would like to express my gratitude to Pinky and Virginia Harrington for reviewing the manuscript and suggesting ways in which it could be—and has been—improved; also to Gary C. Grassl, America's invaluable Gans scholar, for serving as not only a historical consultant but also as the most careful of copyeditors.

Ivor Noël Hume
December 30, 1995

EDITORS' PREFACE

When Ivor Noël Hume died on February 4, 2017, historical archaeology lost its most celebrated luminary, a great innovator, keen scholar and gifted public speaker on behalf of the discipline as both profession and advocation. But Noël, as he was known familiarly, had already ensured that the results of the last excavation he personally directed, the 1991–93 season at Fort Raleigh National Historic Site, would be carried on to publication by Eric Klingelhofer and Nicholas Luccketti. Both of us had worked for Noël at Colonial Williamsburg and had been among the archaeologists he had brought together to investigate Fort Raleigh. Later, when we formed First Colony Foundation in 2003, Noël became an honorary member of its board. Providing advice about our excavation plans and specific assistance in identifying sixteenth-century ceramics, he witnessed firsthand the results of our fieldwork at Fort Raleigh.

Our investigations have expanded the area of Elizabethan activity at Fort Raleigh, even if they have not yet located the 1585 fort and village. They have, moreover, firmly confirmed Noël's conclusion that the earthwork and adjacent "Science Center" were constructed some distance from the core of the settlement. Future fieldwork will no doubt answer some of the questions raised in this report, and additional hard evidence could well alter its conclusions. After Noël completed the draft in 1995, he sent it others for comments—Jean C. Harrington and Garry Grassl, in particular—and so the present form includes some of the changes they suggested. We have been helped in our editing by our First Colony Foundation colleagues

Beverly (Bly) Straube on artifacts and Phillip Evans on documents. We are also indebted to our partners at the National Park Service's Fort Raleigh National Historic Site, Superintendent David Hallac and Cultural Resource Manager Jami Lanier, without whose support this report could not have been made available to the public.

Nearly the entirety of this report is as Noël left it in draft form. With knowledge that became available only after 1995, we took the decision to alter some of the artifact identifications. We did not add to the existing bibliography, however, and to show Noël's thought process in evaluating conflicting information, we retained his wide-ranging arguments for and against various interpretations, even where First Colony Foundation's investigations led to new and unexpected discoveries. Noël would have approved.

Eric Klingelhofer and Nicholas Luccketti
Vice Presidents of Research
First Colony Foundation

FOREWORD

We are pleased to make available this archeological report by esteemed historical archeologist Ivor Noël Hume, whose excavation of America's first "Science Center" in 1991–93 at Fort Raleigh National Historic Site proved that there is more to tell here than just the story of the famed "lost colony" of 1587. In 1585–86, Sir Walter Raleigh's military colony included scientist Thomas Harriot, who, along with metallurgist Joachim Gans, explored the commercial potential of the area's natural resources. The Science Center discovery at Fort Raleigh builds on earlier archeological efforts to form a clearer picture of the human occupation of this site more than four hundred years ago.

The National Park Service played a pioneering role in the discipline of archeology at historic sites beginning with Jamestown in 1934 and is proud to continue this tradition by supporting archeological explorations at Fort Raleigh National Historic Site. From Jean Carl Harrington's discovery and subsequent reconstruction of the earthen fort in the mid-twentieth century to the most recent reexamination of the Science Center site by First Colony Foundation in 2021, the Fort Raleigh story continues to evolve. Although the remnants of past structures and artifacts are incomplete and fragmentary, they provide tangible links to our past. In this way, archeology adds depth and interest to the study of history. Ivor Noël Hume's report adds another important chapter in the multifaceted history of the Roanoke colonies.

David E. Hallac
Superintendent
Fort Raleigh National Historic Site

FOREWORD

This posthumous publication of Ivor Noël Hume's *First and Lost* offers the reader a detailed examination of many important historical archaeological discoveries at the site of Sir Walter Raleigh's Roanoke Island colonies. It is also well told through the words of an eminent researcher and accomplished writer. The First Colony Foundation, a nonprofit organization dedicated to conducting archaeological and historical research, combined with public education and interpretation, is happy to participate in telling this part of America's beginnings with the attempts to establish English colonies in the 1580s. The foundation is proud that many members of the team guided by Noël Hume in these excavations at Fort Raleigh National Historic Site have continued his legacy with the formation of a research organization and its own research successes.

Phillip W. Evans
President
First Colony Foundation

Introduction

IN SEARCH OF AMERICA'S
FIRST ENGLISH SETTLEMENT

No historic site in the Western Hemisphere has a better claim to being the birthplace of English-speaking America than North Carolina's Roanoke Island. Designated by the National Park Service as the Fort Raleigh National Historic Site, the island's north end was home to three successive groups of English settlers between 1585 and 1588. Although not the first Englishmen to land on North American shores, the groups sent out by Sir Walter Raleigh were among the first who came intending to remain.[1] While the colony is remembered more in popular folklore as the birthplace of Virginia Dare (the first English child born on American soil) than for the turbulence of the colonists' presence, the struggles of the first and the unknown fate of the last colonizing effort provided the cornerstone for English colonization that would take permanent hold at Jamestown nineteen years later. Had the first arrivals' scientific leader, Thomas Harriot, determined that continental America's natural resources were not worth exploiting, English competition with Spain would have been delayed, perhaps too long for it to be successful.

The Roanoke ventures are usually categorized as romantic failures, but in truth, they succeeded. Thomas Harriot's *A Briefe and True Report of the New Found Land of Virginia*, first published in 1588—while the third colonizing effort was assumed to be prospering—assured would-be investors that together, patience and pennies "may returne you profit and gaine; bee it either by inhabiting & planting or otherwise in furthering thereof."[2] Uncertainty about the English intent and the whereabouts of the colonists put Spain on the defensive and deterred it from expanding to the Chesapeake, a move that could have shifted Jamestown and Virginia far to the north and thus changed the course of American history. To that extent, therefore, the Roanoke settlements served their purpose and merit a more positive place than most historians have allowed.

In spite of negativism that began as early as 1586 and caused Harriot to complain about the "divers and variable reportes with some slanderous and shamefull speeches bruited abroad, by many that returned from thence," the story of the Lost Colony and its predecessors has intrigued visitors to the site from the seventeenth century to the present day.[3] Archaeologists, both amateur and professional, have dug there on and off since 1895, and across the centuries, souvenir hunters have carried away everything from coins to a glass ball of mercury. Thus, the renewed excavations conducted under the auspices of the Virginia Company Foundation between 1991 and 1993, which are the subject of this study, are but the latest chapter in the site's long history of disturbance.[4]

The discipline today known as historical archaeology had no name when Talcott Williams, an amateur antiquary from Philadelphia, dug the first scientifically motivated holes into the site. By the late 1940s, when the National Park Service undertook its first excavations, the process had come to be known as historic sites archaeology. Because *historic* implied historical importance, and because not everything left us from the past can claim preeminence, in 1967, the name was changed to historical archaeology— meaning the archaeology of sites dating from periods known to us through written history. But digging in the ground and the study of the mute artifacts recovered from it can rarely, if ever, compete with the written word. In 1955, Park Service archeologist Jean C. Harrington dubbed archaeology an auxiliary science to American history,[5] and eight years later, in Raleigh, North Carolina, this writer delivered an address titled "Archaeology: Handmaiden to History."[6] Both, albeit one more flowery than the other, stressed archaeology's secondary role in the interpretation of history. Never was that subsidiary role more demonstrable than in the study of the Fort Raleigh site on Roanoke Island. Consequently, it is necessary first to outline the sequence of events that, to a lesser or greater extent, had an impact on what has been found in the ground and on what might or might not be there to find in the future.

Chapter 1

AMADAS TO WHITE

A Historical Summary

With King Philip's fleets shipping the riches of the Aztec and Incan empires back to Spain, and with England's efforts to reach the Orient via a northeast passage stalled in the Nova Zemblan ice, it was natural that Elizabethan merchants should look west across the Atlantic toward the mystery continent and "discover, search, finde out, and view such remote, heathen and barbarous lands, countreis, and territories, not actually possessed of any Christian prince, nor habited by Christian people."[7] That was the mandate granted to the yet-to-be-knighted Walter Raleigh by Queen Elizabeth on March 25, 1584, a sweeping patent akin to another previously granted to his half-brother Sir Humphrey Gilbert, also of only six years' duration. On April 27, 1884, two ships described as "barkes" set sail from Plymouth bound for the New World. In command (called the Admiral) was Philip Amadas and captaining his support vessel, Arthur Barlowe. Although neither ship is named, Professor David Quinn has suggested that they were the bark *Raleigh* and the pinnace *Dorothy*, both vessels owned by Walter Raleigh. They arrived off the Outer Banks of modern North Carolina on the fourth of July to plant the seeds of British America, which, in patriot minds, would end exactly 192 years later.

Landing on a shore 120 miles north from the first sighting, Amadas and Barlowe "took possession of the same, in the right of the Queenes most excellent Majestie."[8] Entering Pamlico Sound, probably at Wococon Inlet, they remained there for two days before encountering "any people of the Countrey."[9] On the third day, three men in a canoe rowed between the

The arrival of the English at Roanoke Island, from Theodore de Bry's 1590 edition of Thomas Harriot's *A Briefe and True Report*. The original drawing was attributed by De Bry to John White in 1585. *Public domain.*

ships and the island shore, landed one of their number there and waited for a delegation led by Amadas, Barlowe and pilot Simon Ferdinando to go ashore to meet them. After exchanging greetings comprehended by neither recipient, the Native spokesman agreed to go aboard the *Raleigh*, where he was given a shirt and hat and invited to drink wine and eat meat. In return for this hospitality, the Indian went fishing and quickly landed enough to fill his canoe, which catch he shared between the cooks of both bark and pinnace—to the pleasurable amazement of the English explorers.

The next day, led by the weroance (noble) Granganimeo, a company of forty or more Indians visited the ships. Barlowe described them as "very handsome, and goodly people, and in their behaviour as mannerly, and civill, as any of Europe."[10] Through the next several days, trade developed between visitors and residents: food and hides were offered by the Indians in exchange for tin (then an alternative term for pewter) plates, axes, hatchets and knives. They would have preferred swords but were told that they were not for sale. Reassured by what the Indians considered advantageous trading, Granganimeo boarded the admiral, as did his wife, two daughters and a handful of retainers. Forty more waited on the beach; the most senior "had pendants of copper, hanging in every eare," a detail that did not escape English attention. As for the king (chief), he wore on his head "a broade plate of golde, or copper, for being unpolished we knew not what metall it should be."[11]

That Barlowe and his associates should fail to recognize the difference between copper and gold stretches credulity. It is quite likely, therefore, that all knew that the crown was of copper, but Barlowe or Raleigh and his backers wanted a means to put the Midas word in the minds of potential investors. No less reassuring was Barlowe's conclusion that he "found the people most gentle, loving, and faithful, void of all guile, and treason, and such as lived after the manner of the golden age."[12]

Scholars who contend that artist and later governor John White was a key player in all the Roanoke colonizing efforts have suggested that he was a member of the 1584 expedition and therefore a guiding influence in all that was to come. He, however, was not among the leadership "of the companie" listed by Barlowe at the end of his discourse, and there is no reason to doubt that Amadas and Barlowe (both of whom were employees of Walter Raleigh) were capable of assessing Virginia's natural resources. Although overshadowed by Thomas Harriot's famed *Briefe and True Report of the New Found Land of Virginia*, Barlowe's account was rich in anthropological observation, provided relatively accurate descriptions of the natural geography and reported locations of the Indian villages, as well as listing the sighted wildlife and timber.

Having debriefed his captains and having heard the good news, Raleigh "immediatelie prepared for a second viage, which with all expedition (nothing at all regarding the charges that it would amount unto) did presently set in hand."[13] A contemporary described Raleigh as a "gentleman from his infancie brought up and trained in martiall discipline."[14] The seventeenth-century biographer John Aubrey described him as "a tall handsome, and bold man; but his blemish was that he was damnably proud."[15] Although quarrelsome, and a thorn in the sides of military colleagues in Ireland when he chose to be so, Raleigh was able to charm and persuade friends and neighbors into supporting his American voyages. Aubrey recalled that he had persuaded a young friend, Sir Charles Snell, to underwrite the cost of building a ship for his final expedition, a venture that cost the friend "the manner [manor] of Yatton Keynell, the farm at Easton Piers, Thornhill and the church-lease of Bishops Canning."[16] Raleigh turned to people like Snell as he planned his second expedition to Virginia.

To try to define what Raleigh had in mind as he put that expedition together is the only means we have of reading beyond the formalized written mandate given to him under his first patent. Although the authority to get on with the process of discovery and settlement was of only six years' duration, the lands found and settled within that time were to remain Raleigh's and his heirs' and assigns' in perpetuity, requiring only that one fifth of all discovered or later mined "oare of golde and silver" would belong to the Crown.[17] Unlike later patents that called for the Christianizing of native populations, Raleigh received no such instruction beyond requiring that all who were to participate in the enterprise "live together in Christian peace" and that none should be allowed to oppose "the true Christian faith, now professed in the Church of England."[18]

Raleigh almost certainly had little regard for the souls of those whom Christians called savages, for his views of the great and incomprehensible God were more akin to those of many a modern thinker than to the ecclesiastically correct of the Elizabethan age.[19] Although unjustly accused of atheism, Raleigh is better described as skeptical of the established church's moral injunctions. Suffice it to say, therefore, that spreading the Christian word was not primary among Raleigh's New World aspirations. Then again, it is overly simplistic to claim that he was initially motivated by a supposed political and military need to prevent further Spanish expansion on the American continent. In spite of almost a century of New World exploration, little was known about the American mainland, and in the eyes of many, it was primarily a barrier to be crossed or circumnavigated on the way to the riches of the Orient.

Raleigh's interest was primarily in profit, and it mattered little whether it came from the Far East or from the more immediate West. Although a court favorite and the beneficiary of his sovereign's largesse, Walter Raleigh came from a respectable but far from rich West Country family. John Aubrey described him as being "a person so immersed in action all along and in fabrication of his own fortunes (till his confinement in the Tower), could have but little time to study, but what he could spare in the morning."[20] Aubrey also noted "that in his youth for several years he was under straits for want of money" and told how at Oxford, Raleigh had borrowed a gown from a fellow student and neither returned nor paid for it.[21] That even in his years of wealth and prestige Raleigh considered profit as pertinent as patriotism was demonstrated when a 1602 American expedition sponsored by the Earl of Southampton returned with cargoes of sassafras that Raleigh confiscated at portside, citing the terms of his patent that anything Englishmen found in unoccupied America belonged to him.[22]

That Raleigh's second expedition to North Carolina (that of 1585) was manned primarily by people defined as soldiers has led some historians to use this fact as evidence of militaristic intent and, by extension, an intentional warning to Spain. One must remember, however, that Raleigh had personal experience of imposing English will on a native (and in his eyes savage) population through campaigning in Ireland in 1580. It was logical and necessary, therefore, that if he was to obtain whatever America had to offer in gold, silver or even sassafras, his minions should be prepared to take it by force.

Chance and contrary winds ensured that by the time the fleet under the command of Sir Richard Grenville reached the West Indies, the number of would-be settlers had been reduced to a company close to the hundred that Raleigh had taken with him to Ireland in 1580 to help put down Spanish-supported rebels. A listed head count of the vanguard of his American colonists numbered 118, a figure akin to the number of those that would later sail under Virginia Company sponsorship to Jamestown and to Fort St. George on the Kennebec.[23] Professor David Quinn has estimated that of the 118, half were soldiers.[24] The intent, nevertheless, was to expand the colony quickly to as many as six hundred, and equipping three hundred soldiers was a costly undertaking. It is, however, not the cost but the onetime presence of such equipment that has a potential bearing on the archaeological record.

An anonymous advisor writing to Thomas Cavendish (who commanded the 1585 expedition's fifty-ton *Elizabeth*) proposed a military force of eight hundred men, whom he would divide as follows:

> *Fyrst 400. harquebusiers.* [musketeers]
> *Then 100. swordes and lyght moddena targets.* [round shields]
> *Then 150. long bows*
> *Then 100. Armed men with millan corselettes lyght.*
> *Then 50. Armed men with lyght Corsellettes with short weapons.*

The advisor explained that he chose the light armor "for they are to dealt with naked men." He proposed that one hundred men should always be on duty in the fort and that "all the rest should labor by turns tyll the forte be Ended."[25]

Because this study is designed to focus on the Fort Raleigh site, it is irrelevant to dwell on events relating to the 1585 voyage and to exploratory expeditions led by Grenville upon his arrival. I will only note that in short order, and on Grenville's instructions, Philip Amadas turned Indians whom he and Barlowe had previously found "gentle, loving, and faithful" into disillusioned, wary and vengeful foes.[26]

It would, of course, be a grave mistake to lump all the Indians together (as, indeed, Raleigh and his stay-at-home adventurers may well have done). Grenville's heavy-handed approach to tribes living on the mainland to the southwest of Pamlico Sound evidently drew approval from others living to the north and on Roanoke Island, where the colonists first settled in harmony with the followers of their island neighbor, the senior weroance Wingina. It is no less important to recall that when Amadas and Barlowe returned to

England in 1584, they had taken two Indians with them: Wanchese from the Roanokes and Manteo from the Croatoan tribe that lived at the south end of Hatteras Island and on the adjacent Ocracoke Island. Although Wanchese would ally himself with the the colonists' enemies, Manteo was to remain a friend whose loyalty eventually secured him the questionable honor of becoming England's first vassal king in America.

To the modern Outer Banks visitor or resident, the ocean-fronting barrier is a sound-protecting wall broken only by Oregon, Hatteras and Ocracoke Inlets. But in the sixteenth and later centuries, the sand barrier was breached by more than twice that number, the deepest at Wococon (Ocracoke). It was through this inlet that Grenville steered his ships—grounding the *Tiger* in the process. Roanoke Island lies about sixty miles to the north of Wococon Inlet, and although approachable through perhaps three much closer inlets, all were shallow and shoaled—providing too little water for vessels above the size of a pinnace to reach the island's shores. This meant that it was not easily invaded by a large force but also that if such a magnum enemy should approach, settlers on the island would be slow to learn of its approach and hard put to escape. If, as has been suggested, the intent was to establish a base from which to attack Spanish treasure ships on the *flotas*' usual course, then Roanoke Island had to have been the least appropriate locale from which to operate.

The decision to settle on Roanoke evidently was the by-product of the Amadas and Barlowe visit of 1584 and influenced by the belief that with the somewhat Anglicized Manteo and Wanchese returning aboard the fleet and the assurance that the natives were friendly, the island would be a safe and satisfactory base from which to explore. Furthermore, once Grenville and his transporting fleet had sailed away, it was unlikely that passing Spaniards would ever know that the English were there.[27]

The homebound fleet departed on August 25, and nine days later, Governor Ralph Lane sent by the remaining ship a letter to Richard Hakluyt the elder, one of England's principal proponents of westerly expansion, assuring him that all was well and addressing his letter from the "new Fort in Virginia." Lane made it clear that the neighboring "Savages were naturally most curteous & very desirous to have clothes, but especially of coarse cloth rather than silk." Lane's explorers had already crossed to the mainland and found it to be "the goodliest soil under the cope of heaven," with clay suitable for pharmaceutical use that Lane termed "Terra Samia, otherwise Terra sigillata."[28] Earlier in the same letter, Lane had mentioned the abundance of "many sortes of Apothecarie drugs."[29] In his September 8 letter from the fort, Lane mentioned the

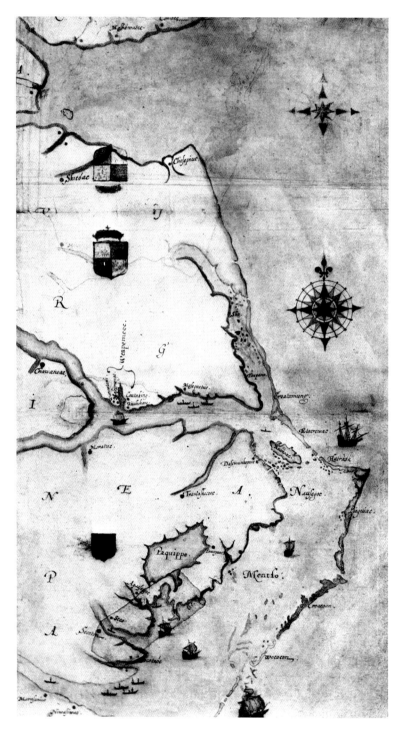

The Harriot and White map of Virginia completed after the return to England of Ralph Lane's colonists in 1586. © *The Trustees of the British Museum.*

availability of wheat that "yealde the bothe corne, and sugar, whereof our Physycyan here hath sente an assaye to our Lord Sir Walter Rawlleye."[30] In an earlier letter to the secretary of state written before Grenville's fleet sailed home, Lane noted that a preliminary survey had yielded "soo many, soo rare, and soo singulare commodytyes (by the unyversalle opynyone both of our Appotycaryes and all our merchantes here) as to justify confidence in the queen's new kingedom of Verginia."[31]

The identity of the apothecaries and merchants remains uncertain, and it is indeed surprising that Lane failed here to name either Thomas Harriot or "mineralman" Joachim Gans, though his later discourse of the 1585–86 colony does refer to "Master Yougham" in reference to copper.[32] Harriot is numbered among the great minds of Elizabethan England; oceanographer, astronomer, mathematician and occasional alchemist, he was as close as an Englishman came to being a European renaissance man. His *Briefe and True Report* is an essay in botany, mineralogy, pharmacy, anthropology and zoology and exhibits a broad knowledge also of the commonplace. Thus, for example, in describing potential uses for cedarwood, he pointed out that it would be applicable "for Chests, Boxes, Bedsteedes, Lutes, Virginals, and many things els."[33]

There is no doubt that the scholarly Harriot had a strong influence on Walter Raleigh, and if biographer John Aubrey is to be believed, Harriot's religious beliefs are likely to have influenced his employer's. Wrote Aubrey:

> *He made a philosophical theology, wherein he cast off the Old Testament, and then the new one would (consequently) have no foundation. He was Deist. His doctrine he taught to Sir Walter Raleigh, Henry, earl of Northumberland, and some others. The divines of those times looked on his manner of death as a judgment upon him for valuing the Scripture at nothing.*[34]

Raleigh would later introduce Harriot to Henry, ninth earl of Northumberland, who was so impressed by his learning and affability that he granted him a lifelong annual stipend of £300. In 1606, after both Raleigh and Northumberland had been imprisoned in the Tower, Harriot became a frequent visitor and scientific consultant, and along with two other mathematicians, Robert Hues and Walter Warner, "became one of the earl of Northumberland's three Magi."[35] In short, Thomas Harriot possessed the mind and the learning needed to assess the economic viability of Virginia.

With Harriot, and as senior metallurgist, went the Jewish Joachim Gans, a native of Prague and a specialist in copper smelting who had been invited to settle in England. He helped upgrade the antiquated copper industry at Keswick in the county of Cumberland. Here the Company of Mines Royal had been established in 1564. Four years later, it was renamed and incorporated by assent of Queen Elizabeth as the Society of Mines Royal. The art and mystery of metallic mining was then considered a German skill, and thus the Keswick establishment was manned by Germans and run by Daniel Hochstetler of Augsburg. Later, in the winter of 1589–90, Raleigh's former metallurgist translated and edited book 5 of Lazarus Ercker's *Treatise on Ores and Essays* for Sir Francis Walsingham, the Queen's principal secretary.

Although Gans was born in today's Czeck Republic, this was part of the Holy Roman Empire ruled by the Hapsburgs, and he was considered a German or, more commonly, a Dutch (or Deutsch) man.[36] His date of birth is unknown but usually is attributed to the mid-sixteenth century—which may have made him a few years older than Harriot. In how close a physical proximity Gans and Harriot worked has gone unrecorded, and the latter in his *Briefe and True Report* does not mention Gans by name, nor does Harriot describe either the place or the conditions under which they worked. It is reasonable to deduce, however, that both men took with them scientific equipment then considered state of the art.

Harriot derived satisfaction from amazing the Indians with the array and capabilities of his instruments. "Most things they sawe with us," he wrote, "as mathematicall instruments, sea compasses, the vertue of the loadstone in drawing yron, a perspective glasse whereby was shewed manie strange sightes, burning glasses, wildfire woorkes, gunnes, bookes, writing and reading, spring clocks that seeme to goe of themselves, and manie other things that wee had."[37]

In trying to assess what it was like to have lived on Roanoke Island with Raleigh's colonists—which, after all, is the purpose of historical archaeology—it is necessary not only to comb through the directly related records but also to seek likely paralleling information from collateral sources. Thus, for example, the inventory and charges for supplies taken with Martin Frobisher

Print made by Francis Delaram, circa 1620, very similar to the alleged portrait of Thomas Harriot (1560–1621) in the collection of Trinity College, Oxford. It has also been considered that of John Napier of Merchiston and is so inventoried by the British Museum (BM P,1.216). *Public domain.*

in his 1576 search for the Northwest Passage are doubtless similar to those carried by any exploratory endeavor. The fleet's surgeon, Arnold Langly, was paid £2. 13s 4d for a chest full of surgery wares—a kit that almost certainly included tin-enameled albarelli drug pots comparable to fragments that would be found on the Fort Raleigh site (see the image on page 136). Then again, one knows that to smelt and refine as well as to assay his metal, Gans would have needed a forge and a pair of blacksmith's bellows. The Frobisher inventory does not reveal how big they would have been or how much was leather and how much wood, but it does give a clue to their value: "paid to good wife Brighte smythe Followithe for a great pare of bellowes for smythes forge" fifteen shillings, or a little more than a quarter of the value of the surgeon's chest.[38]

There was, of course, a significant difference between the first Frobisher voyage and that of Raleigh's first colonizing effort. Thanks to Amadas and Barlowe, Grenville and Lane knew where they were going. Frobisher had hoped to reach China or Japan and the civilized nobility that ruled there. Thus, for example, his inventory of costs included payments to a scribe for translating "the Quenes majesties Letter of Favour" from Latin into Greek and for penning copies in Latin, to another for drawing the ornamental capital letters and outlining the queen's portrait and to yet another for "culleringe in the quenes Majesties pictures therin," plus additional charges for the parchment, for the "brode seal of England" and for boxes to contain the impressive-appearing documents.[39] Raleigh's men needed no such diplomatic support (at more than double the price of the surgeon's chest); their negotiations were not to be with gold-appareled princes but with naked "salvages" ready to sell their birthright for a bag of beads or a parcel of kitchen knives.

Another pertinent ancillary record recalls instructions set out in 1582 or 1583 for a planned northerly voyage by Sir Humphrey Gilbert. In this record are instructions to the expedition's artist and mapmaker Thomas Bavin, who was never to "go at any tyme without a payer of writing Tables." Along with sea instruments and a "flate watch clock" that would go for twenty-four or forty hours without winding, Bavin was to take with him

a good store of parchments, Paper Ryall, Quills, and Inck, black powder to make yncke, and of all sortes of colours to drawe all things to life, gumme, pensyll, a stone to grind Colours, mouth glue, black leade, 2 payres of brazen Compasses, And other Instruments to drawe cardes and plottes.[40]

John White's 1585 watercolor drawing of the Indian village of Secoton. © *The Trustees of the British Museum.*

The Roanoke voyages' premier authority, David Beers Quinn, has been among the many who contend that Raleigh's parallel to Thomas Bavin as artist and mapmaker was John White, the man destined to lead the third expedition and who would return in 1590 in search of his lost colony. There is no denying that White was in Virginia in the summer of 1585 when he drew and painted the watercolors that are his incomparable legacy to American history and anthropology, but there is no direct evidence—other than geese and swans in his paintings, which may have spent the full year there in the colder sixteenth century—that he remained with Lane after Grenville sailed for home.[41] On the contrary, the folio that contains his drawings is dated 1585 and not 1586.[42]

The scant surviving evidence shows that White was among those who, on July 11, 1585, accompanied Grenville on his tour of Pamlico Sound and the rivers flowing into it.[43] It was then that White made his drawings of Pomeioc and Secoton and of their Algonquian inhabitants, drawings that unquestionably went home with Grenville's fleet. The absence of any drawings of the settlement on Roanoke Island or of the fauna and flora of that region—subjects so well covered on the voyage prior to Grenville's departure—has been explained as the result of losses suffered when Lane and his settlers made a hasty departure in June 1586.[44] There being no documents naming White to support that conclusion, the evidence of his drawings' cover sheet makes it infinitely more likely that White (whose name is absent from the listing of those who remained with Lane "one whole yeere in Virginia") went home with the fleet. One may reasonably conclude, therefore, that the observatory and cartographic duties assigned to Bavin would have been shouldered by the eminently able Thomas Harriot. That the British Museum's John White collection includes a map of Virginia containing details unknown when Grenville departed in August 1585 is explainable by a White/Harriot collaboration after the latter returned in 1586.[45] The conclusion, therefore, may reasonably be that the content of the Virginia map is attributable to Harriot (see the figure on page 33). There is, however, no evidence that Harriot was an artist capable of drawing people, places or things, and in that respect, he must have supplied the basic cartographic material for White to copy and add details: e.g., ships and canoes.

It is clear that relations between Grenville and Lane had deteriorated to crisis point well before the 1585 fleet departed and that in the taking sides that ensued, it is possible that White chose not to remain.[46] Be that as it may, the only significant factor is the absence of any White-drawn elevation or plan to show what the "Newe Forte in Verginia" looked like or where it was located. For that, therefore, historians are forced to rely on the sometimes questionable testimony of the archaeologist's trowel. But before addressing the evidence from the earth, it is necessary first to examine in detail the few documentary clues to the character of Lane's settlement and defenses. No less pertinent is the sequence of events that followed his departure and led to John White's brief return in 1590.

Much has been made of White's sketches both of the Grenville expedition's temporary base at Guayanilla Bay in Puerto Rico (St. John's Island) built and occupied in May 1585 and of his rendering of elaborate fortifications erected around two piles of pilfered Spanish salt on a Puerto Rican beach. In the words of Paul Hulton, retired deputy keeper in the Department of Prints and Drawings at the British Museum, "The design of the fort has close affinities with Fort Raleigh on Roanoke Island, excavated and reconstructed (1947–50)."[47] Although much later archaeological evidence would show that this perceived affinity was coincidental, it is significant that Roanoke's Ralph Lane had been in command of the raid on the salt supplies and would have been responsible for building the surrounding defenses. The anonymous author of a report of the Grenville expedition described how he went to Roxo Bay (at Cabo Rojo) and "as soon as hee arrived there, hee landed with his men to the number of 20, and intrenched himselfe upon the sandes immediately, compassing one of their salt hils within the trench."[48]

This deponent evidently did not accompany Lane, and therefore, his testimony may rely solely on what Lane subsequently reported. Nevertheless, there is an evident discrepancy, in that White's watercolor shows two salt piles within the trenched defenses and not the reported "one of their salt hils." The clear-cut elaboration of the entrenchments far more closely resembles textbook illustrations in manuals of military engineering than it does the hurried digging-in of a handful of salt snatchers.[49] With that in mind, one may legitimately wonder whether White was there and whether instead he, too, based his interpretation on Lane's subsequent reporting. All that can safely be said is that on arriving at the salt site, Lane "intrenched himselfe." That indisputable fact has been used to suggest that he had a special interest in the construction of earthworks and so would have built in a like manner on Roanoke Island.

Unlike the Guayanilla Bay defenses that embraced all the shore-built structures, the Roanoke Island settlement appears to have been constructed on the Northern Irish bawn village plan—an open village defended by a small fort into which the inhabitants could flee when attacked. Describing a planned Indian assault, Lane recounted how

John White's 1585 watercolor drawing of Ralph Lane's temporary beach defenses at Cape Rojo, Puerto Rico. © *The Trustees of the British Museum.*

in the dead time of the night they would have beset my house, and put fire in the reedes that the same was covered with: meaning (as it was likely) that my selfe would have come running out of a sudden amazed in my shirt without armes, upon the instant whereof they would have knocked out my braines. The same order, Lane went on, was given to certain of his fellows [the Indians Tarraquine and Andacon], *for M. Heriots,—so for all the rest of our better sort, all our houses at one instant being set on fire as afore is saide, and that as well of them of the fort, as for us at the towne.*[50]

From the foregoing description one learns several important facts. First, as previously noted, the town was separated from the fort, but unlike the Irish precedent, the senior officials did not reside within the fort. Lane and the colleagues he called "our better sort" lived together in the "towne" in reed-thatched houses. That these colleagues included very senior people (e.g., discoverer Philip Amadas), whom Lane did not name as specific targets, prompts the question: Why, then, were some Indians (the "certaine of his fellowes") assigned to single out Harriot from all the rest?

The answer, as archaeology would eventually suggest, was that Harriot's house and scientific center were located apart from the village and would be targeted by a separate troop of Indians.

The spring of 1586 found Lane and his settlers cut off from food trade with the Indians and in a virtual state of war with them, fast running short of all manner of supplies, and waiting impatiently for the arrival of Grenville's reinforcements. In June, an approaching fleet was sighted but proved to be that of Sir Francis Drake returning from a piratical excursion through the Spanish Caribbean. He brought with him hardware looted from St. Augustine and points south, as well as a labor force comprising Turkish and North African slaves and Central American Indians seized from Spanish masters. But he brought no food and was short of it himself. Many details of the negotiations between Lane, his officers and Drake are wanting, but the colonists determined to accept Drake's offer of the seventy-ton bark *Francis*, which would remain to bring them home if Grenville failed to arrive before their position became untenable. Drake also would leave two pinnaces and four smaller boats along with supplies of firearms ("calievers"), ammunition, bladed weapons and clothing. Unfortunately, an approaching hurricane scattered the fleet, driving the *Francis* to sea with several of Lane's top men aboard. When the storm abated, Drake's ships reassembled and his officers could review the damage and losses, Drake offered Lane another vessel, the bark *Bonner*, double the tonnage of the *Francis*. But that asset was also its disadvantage. The *Bonner* drew too much water to pass over the shoals into the safety of the sounds. Consequently, Lane made a hurried decision to take his people home with Drake—so hurried, in fact, that three men on the mainland were left behind.

The speed at which the settlers packed up and left the "Newe Forte in Verginia" can only be guessed at; nevertheless, determining what they took provides a clue to what they left behind. Lane told how Drake sent

> *his Pinnesses unto our island for the fetching away of the few that were there left with our baggage, the weather was so boisterous, & the pinnesses so often on ground, that the most of all we had, with all our Cards, Books and writings were by the Sailers cast overboord, the greater number of the fleet being much agrieved with their long and dangerous abode in that miserable road.*[51]

From that account grew the legend that John White had seen a year's worth of invaluable drawings thrown overboard by Drake's unhappy sailors. Harriot, however, who along with Gans was the most closely identified with the expedition's scientific record, said nothing about White's anguish or his losses—or indeed about his presence. Instead, he focused on a string of pearls that had been assembled as a gift to Queen Elizabeth "had wee not by casualtie and through extremity of a storme, lost them with many things els in comming away from the countrey."[52]

One may argue that most of the "other sort" had few possessions besides their weapons and the clothes on their backs and so had little to leave behind, while those of the "better sort" made sure everything that mattered to them got packed. An anonymously authored summary of Drake's stay recalled how, in their eagerness to be gone, the colonists, fearing that they "should be left behinde they left all things confusedly, as if they had been chased from thence by a mighty army.[53] As for the builders' hardware and other useful loot brought north for Raleigh's people, most if not all of that must have been still aboard when the storm broke and almost certainly remained there while the future of the colony continued in dispute. It is safe to deduce, therefore, that heavy equipment like Gans's blacksmith's bellows would have been left behind along with nonmilitary tools, kitchen pots and pans, and everything that was built on the island, from houses to bedsteads and all other domestic furniture, remained both in the "towne" and in the fort. It is equally fair to assume that within hours of the colonists' departure, Indians invaded the settlement and began to carry off everything they could load aboard canoes.[54]

Several days after Drake's fleet had passed below the horizon, the first relief vessel arrived, "a ship of an hundred tunne, fraighted with all maner of things in most plentifull maner, for the supply and reliefe of [Raleigh's] Colony"—but which, upon finding no one, returned with "all the aforesayd provision to England."[55] Two weeks later, Grenville's fleet of three ships arrived and found "the places which they inhabited desolate."[56] From the testimony of Grenville's Portuguese pilot Pedro Diaz, one learns that the searchers found two hanging corpses, one an Englishman and the other an Indian, but who they were and why and when they died has gone unrecorded. More pertinent is Diaz's statement in his 1589 deposition to the Spaniards in Havana that on the island, Lane's people had built "a wooden fort of little strength…on the inside by the water."[57]

Believing that Lane's "Newe Forte" was an earthwork akin to White's rendering of the salt hill defenses on the Puerto Rican shore, historians have had much trouble with Diaz's statement that the Roanoke structure was of wood.[58] Attention is drawn, therefore, to Diaz's own admission that Grenville did not trust him to go on shore or enter the fort.[59] That being so, it is argued, Diaz had only someone else's word that Lane's fort was of wood and poorly built. According to Diaz's testimony, Grenville remained

Richard Schlecht's sketch of the flight of Ralph Lane's colonists to Drake's waiting fleet. *Sketch by Richard Schlecht.*

off the Outer Banks for two weeks, at first searching for Lane's company and then establishing a small garrison in their vacated settlement to hold the territory for England. Eighteen (or perhaps fifteen) men were to remain with supplies to last a year. Also left with them were four pieces of cast-iron artillery. This last item is curious, for it assumes that Grenville's garrison had lacked ordnance. What then, one might reasonably inquire, had become of the artillery that had defended Lane's fort and that would have been too heavy to have been loaded aboard Drake's crowded pinnaces?[60]

There is no evidence that Grenville provided his men with a newly built palisade or with a freshly dug earthwork wherein to mount their four cast-iron guns. However, it certainly is possible that he used seamen and carpenters from the anchored flotilla to assist in that way.[61] All too often, the surviving documentation relies on secondary and even tertiary sources—self-serving descriptions by people like Diaz or information garnered from Indians and later set down in wording that almost certainly changed in transmission. Knowledge of the fate of Grenville's garrison comes from just such a dubious source, being told to the 1587 colonists by Croatoan Indians who undoubtedly heard it from neighbors who had been responsible for what happened.

The Indians' narrative put the total number of colonists at fifteen rather than Diaz's eighteen and stated that of those, only eleven were in and around "the houses where our men carelesly lived" when attacked by some thirty Indians. With one man dead by a blow from a wooden sword, the rest

> *were forced to take* [to] *the house, wherein all their victuall, and weapons were: but the Savages foorthwith set the same on fire: by meanes wherof our men were forced to take such weapons as came first to hand, and without order to runne foorth among the Savages, with whom they skirmished above an howre. In this skirmish another of our men was shotte in the mouth with an arrow, where he died: and also one of the Savages was shot in the side by one of our men, with a wild fire arrow, whereof he died presently.*

The narrative went on to state that:

> *The place where they fought was of great advantage to the Savages, by meanes of the thicke trees, behinde which the Savages through their nimblenes, defended themselves, and so offended our men with their arrowes, that our men being some of them hurt, retyred fighting to the water side where their boat lay, with which they fled towards Hatorask.*

On the way, the survivors picked up the four who had been absent and continued south to land on a small island flanking Hatorask (Port Ferdinando), "where they remayned a while, but afterward departed, whither as yet we know not."[62]

The "we" referred to above was John White and his fellow settlers who had arrived in Raleigh's bigger and better expedition that had reached Hatteras Island on July 22, 1587, and the next day went ashore on Roanoke Island. The account of Grenville's lost garrison evidently was obtained from Manteo, who spoke English and who, in spite of mounting evidence that the English were no more to be trusted than any neighboring rival, remained their spokesman, mediator and friend. How (or if) Manteo knew that the embattled garrison had skirmished "above an howre" before fleeing to the waterside is just another of Roanoke Island's lesser mysteries. Other details, however, could have been checked, and it is unlikely that, even if told, White would have reported that trees were thick in the vicinity of the store if such was not the case.

The account has been studied in infinite detail and can be read to support differing theories as to where the storehouse stood and where the colonists' boat lay. Did they fight for an hour amid the trees adjacent to the burned store, or did it take them an hour to reach the safety of their boat, and how many of those sixty minutes were spent skirmishing and how many in flight? These are all questions whose answers would have a bearing on the placement of Lane's village in relationship to the waterside moorings or jetty. More valuable than the Indians' hearsay is the evidence of John White's own eyes when, on July 23, he entered Ralph Lane's abandoned and almost certainly looted village with its "forte" and "sundry necessary and decent houses. When we came thither," wrote White, "we found the fort rased down, but all the houses standing unhurt, saving that the neather rooms of them, and also of the forte, were overgrown with melons of divers sortes."[63] Although White is usually assumed to have been returning to the village he had occupied for a year and to the house wherein he had lived, his journal gives no hint of recognition or any regret that things he had left behind had been broken or carried away by the Indians.[64]

How, one may ask, could White have inspected the settlement and found all (not some, but all) the houses unhurt when he, himself, recounted the burning of the Grenville garrison's storehouse? How could its ruined shell— and, presumably, the calcinated stores and weapons that had been in it—have escaped his notice? Again, there is no answer, any more than there is a certain and correct interpretation of what White meant by finding the fort "rased

The escape of Grenville's garrison in 1586. *Sketch by Richard Schlecht.*

downe." The verb can mean "dismantled," "demolished" and "collapsed," and being reportedly of wood and of "little strength" in the summer of 1586, the palisade may well have fallen apart by the following year. Then again, it may have been deliberately dismantled by Grenville's seamen if the structure was thought to have become a liability rather than an asset. Whatever the interpretation, one can safely conclude that when White arrived with his hundred and more men, women and children, no fortified retreat awaited them. Immediately, however, orders were given that "every man should be employed for the repayring of those houses, which wee found standing, and also to make other new Cottages, for such as should need."[65]

It is safe to conclude that White's colonists were to repair and occupy Lane's open and undefended village houses and that if more were needed, new structures were to be erected. At this point, however, sixteenth-century semantics again intrude. What, one must inquire, was meant by "cottages"? An expansion of the word *cot*, the primary definitions of *cottage* are a "dwelling house of small size and humble character" and "a small temporary erection used for shelter; a cot, hut, shed, etc."[66] Unfortunately for archaeologists and historians, there is a significant difference between a small house of intended permanence and a temporary cot, hut or shed. If the latter was White's intent, however, the erection of temporary huts may be construed as a reflection of the fact that Raleigh's colony was not expected to remain on Roanoke Island but rather to head north to establish the "Cittie of Ralegh" on a shore of the Chesapeake.

Although White had intended to return to the island, his aim had been to ensure the well-being of Grenville's garrison and immediately to continue northward before his three ships returned to England. Instead, his authority was usurped by the flagship's sailing master, Simon Fernandez, who insisted that it was already too late in the year to move on and that he and the crews intended to sail at once for England. By White's own admission, "it booted not the Governour [White] to contend with them."[67]

Disputes with Fernandez had erupted at the outset of the voyage, and White's journal is replete with charges against him, some of them seemingly picayune and more evidence of White's paranoia than of this experienced officer's mistakes. It is fairly evident, however, that the weakness of White's leadership boded ill for those who were to remain under his command, and within days of resettling Lane's village, his eleven assistants (the twelfth had already been killed by Indians) were maneuvering to oust him.

On August 22, "the whole company both of the Assistants and planters" called on White to return to England with the ships, the better and sooner to obtain supplies. The account explains at some length his resistance to this request, his argument ending with a fear that his goods might be pilfered if they were carried north to the new location before he could return. He added that he had already "found some proofe" of such thievery after being parted from his possessions for only three days.[68]

After being given a written assurance that those remaining would be held monetarily responsible for White's possessions, three days later, he agreed to go. With him went the last documentation of the activities and eventual fate of Raleigh's second settlement attempt. The looming war with Spain that was to culminate in the 1588 defeat and scattering of Philip II's armada left John White in London vainly pleading for ships and a new supply until 1590, when, with nothing more than his personal baggage, he was able to secure passage aboard the *Moonlight*, the lead ship in a privateering expedition to the Caribbean. His own words make it evident that his was not a dominating personality and that although Raleigh still expressed concern for the well-being of his colonists, raising backing for yet another expedition was not a high priority.

In a study such as this that must focus on the material remains of the Roanoke settlements, only those details necessary to define the sequence and to describe places, artifacts and activities are relevant—no matter how tangentially interesting others may be. Suffice it to say, therefore, that White eventually returned to Roanoke Island on August 16, 1590, and reentered the village where he had left his company—the people who included his own daughter and grandchild. Knowing that their intent had been "to remove from Roanoak 50 miles into the maine," it cannot have surprised him to find the village deserted. Nevertheless, it had changed significantly since last he saw it. The once open settlement, which had begun life protected only by its bawn-style structure of wood and of little strength, now was surrounded with what passed for a city wall.

White found the place, he said, "very strongly enclosed with a high palisado of great trees, with cortynes and flankers very fort-like."[69] But although the palisades were impressively intact, the dwellings they had protected were not. White "found the houses taken downe," by which one might conclude that they had been deliberately dismantled, certainly not burned or fallen into ruin. Thus one has the reverse of the condition that he had reported in 1587 when he found the houses "intact but the fort rased down."

White had thus commented on the "taken downe" houses before he described the palisade of great trees, making it possible to argue that if they were inside the fort, he could not have known that they were gone until he entered the stockade—in which case, that should have been described first. One must remember, however, that White was writing some years *after* the visit and that he may have thought the absence of houses more important or more striking in his memory than was the palisade. On balance, however, it seems logical and most likely, in light of the known Indian hostility, that the wooden walls had, indeed, encompassed the dwellings.

White went on to comment on objects left within the palisade, among them bars of iron, two pigs of lead, iron shot for guns of saker bore and four "yron fowlers." Fowlers were light cannon of the type used aboard ships and could equate with the "one small Quarter-deck-Gun, made of Iron Staves" found on the site in 1701.[70] But then again, one knows that Grenville had left four pieces of artillery, albeit all of them with cast-iron rather than wrought tubes. These, however, were not the only guns White could expect to have found left behind, for he noted that he searched for "the last Falkons and small Ordinance which were left with them, at my departure from them."[71] Heavier than fowlers, falcons were approximately half the size of sakers, whose shot White found within the palisade.

All that was left—or rather, all that White noticed to have been left—were "such like heavie things," a clue of potential value in reconstructing the circumstances under which the colonists departed.[72] They, of course, had left one specific clue and part of another. Before leaving for England, White had instructed his remaining assistants that on departing

> *into the maine (onto the mainland) they should carve on the trees or posts of the dores the name of the place where they should be seated and that if they should happen to be distressed in any of those places, that then they should carve over the letter or name, a cross.*[73]

When White first approached the deserted settlement, he came upon a tree near the shore carved with the letters *CRO*, and when he reached the palisade gate, he found the bark stripped from the post and on it the full name *CROATOAN*—but no distress cross. Naturally enough, White concluded that he had "safely found a certaine token of their safe being at Croatoan, which is the place where Manteo was borne, and the Savages of the Iland our friends."[74] White had expected to return to the ship and sail southward along the coast trying to make contact with the settlers, but as had happened twice before, bad weather demanded a hasty retreat, and so to White's chagrin, he was forced to return to England without again setting foot on American soil.

Before leaving Roanoke Island, White's companions had made a discovery that could bear on future archaeology, but like most of his narrative, from a distance of four centuries, his words are as equivocal as they are helpful. He described how, while returning from "the point of the Creeke" to the settlement site, he was met by some of the sailors, who told him that they had "found where divers chests had bene hidden, and long sithence digged up againe and broken up, and much of the goods in them spoyled and scattered about, but nothing left, of such things as the Savages knew any use of, undefaced. Presently," White continued, "Captain Cooke and I went to the place, which was in the end of an old trench, made two yeeres past by Captain Amadas."

Immediately one is brought up short. Two years prior to August 1590 would have been in the summer of 1588, and collateral evidence from Spanish sources suggests that by July that year, White's colonists had already departed.[75] Besides, Captain Amadas was not among the settlers whom White had brought over in 1587. He had, however, been the senior officer under Lane (and "Admirall of the countrey") in 1585 and 1586. Working under the assumption that Lane's weak wooden fort was actually an earthwork, historian David Quinn has suggested that the old trench had "probably [formed] part of the original fortifications." If true, however, it is surprising that White did not say so.[76]

John White's movements from the creek (and, of course, one asks *which* creek?) back to the settlement and thence to the old trench are recorded with neither direction nor distance, rendering it impossible to know which was where. Previously cited evidence from the narrative of Ralph Lane indicates that Harriot's house was set apart from the main village. One knows, too, that Grenville's burned storehouse that White failed to mention (or notice?) in 1587 was in a wooded sector, but at the same time, White's Indian report spoke of the garrison living carelessly in houses—houses that almost certainly were those of Lane's vacated village. It being highly unlikely that Grenville would have built a separate store to house the garrison's provisions when all of Lane's structures were vacant and available, it must be assumed that the attackers stormed the village, around which the forest stood relatively close. One may also assume that after White's return home, the second group of colonists built a settlement-girdling palisade, cutting down a large number of trees to do so and, at the same time, pruning the forest back beyond— if they were wise—the approximately sixty-foot effective aimed range of a caliver or arquebus.[77]

The topographical questions raised by White's thinly described movements are no less puzzling than is his description of what he saw on reaching the trench:

Wee found five Chests that had bene carefully hidden of the Planters, and of the same chests three were my owne, and about the place many of my things spoyled and broken, and my bookes torne from the covers, the frames of some of my pictures and Mappes rotten and spoyled with rayne, and my

armor almost eaten through with rust; this could bee no other but the deede
of the Savages our enemies at Dasamongwepeuk.[78]

That there were five chests, three of them White's, gives some hint at
the quantity of personal possessions the leadership had brought with them.
Although his armor could have filled one chest, the inference that the others
contained only books and framed pictures and maps is less than plausible.
Indeed, the relative conditions of armor and paper is itself puzzling. The
former is said to have been almost eaten through with rust. In three years,
steel armor would rust—but not to the point of perforation. On the other
hand, in that space of time, the leather straps, canvas linings and velvet
piccadils could easily rot away, rendering the armor unwearable. But that
was not White's complaint. As for his books, once robbed of their covers—
probably by Indians who wanted their decorative brass bosses and clasps—
one would expect the pages to be scattered away from the trench, unless,
of course, they had been thrown back into the opened chests, as well they
might. All that can be said with any assurance is that for the armor to decay
beyond mere surface rust, the breaching of the chests must have occurred
within a year or so of White's 1587 departure. Most surprising, however,
is the fact that the armor was still there, for as he had already noted, the
Indians had carried off all such things as they "knew any use of."

No less puzzling is the reason for the chest's none-too-well-concealed
burial. When urged to return home, White's demurral had been founded
as much upon the safety of his possessions as upon the preservation of his
reputation. Indeed, it was the provision of written assurance that his goods
would be protected and the settlers held monetarily responsible for them that
prompted him to leave. What, then, were the circumstances or the mindset
that prompted his officers to dump their governor's possessions into the end
of an old trench? And whose were the other two chests, and what had they
contained? These, of course, are minor details when compared with the one
that was destined to become one of the greatest unanswered questions in
American history: what became of Sir Walter Raleigh's Lost Colony?

Regardless of the popular assumption that archaeological discoveries
on the island can provide the answer, the fact of the matter is that the
colonists left it. Consequently, it is to some as-yet-unknown location (or
locations) where their journey ended to which archaeologists must turn
for the answer. Until the remains of the settlers and their possessions are
identified, researchers must continue to extract what they can from John
White's frustratingly brief narrative.

The clues that gave him great joy were first the tree-carved *CRO* and then the name *CROATOAN* on the palisade's gatepost. Some have deduced that the destination was written first on the gate and then begun again on the waterside tree, the chipping interrupted before it could be completed—interrupted, perhaps, by an Indian attack that hastened the colonists' departure. No less logical, and possibly more so, is a reverse interpretation: the settlers were in the last stages of an orderly and planned evacuation when somebody remembered White's instruction to leave their destination carved somewhere where it could be found. Shortly after the carver set to work on a waterside tree, someone asked how they could be sure that a returning White would approach from the direction necessary to find the inscription or even to notice the tree. Impressed by the wisdom of that thought, the carver was dispatched back to the settlement to leave the message where no one could miss it. But why southerly Croatoan?

Why not, say, the Indians' Chesepioc equivalent of northerly Virginia Beach? Part of the answer may be found in Ralph Lane's statement that in 1586 he was "enforced to sende Captaine Stafford with 20. with him to Croatoan my Lord Admirals Iland to serve two turnes in one, that is to say, to feede himself and his company, and also to keepe watch if any shipping came upon the coast to warne us of the same."[79] The colonists lacked the boats to carry any of their heavy and bulky possessions, and besides, they would have had to assume that part of their northward journey would be on foot. It made sense, therefore, to leave behind some of their men and one or more of the larger boats to transport the heavy materials down to My Lord Admiral's Island. There, in the safety of the territory of Manteo and his friendly Croatoan Indians, the heavy-duty cadre could await the expected return of White's supply convoy in the spring of 1588. With time on their hands, they may have passed it by dismantling the Roanoke Island houses and salvaging for shipment all the hewn and dressed building materials—thus explaining why White found "the houses taken downe."[80]

Knowing the English propensity for falling foul of their friends and remembering that Manteo was somewhat out of touch with his Native roots, it is possible that the Croatoan colonists outstayed their welcome and were killed either by their disillusioned hosts or by Pomouiks or Secotans from the mainland whom Grenville had alienated in the summer of 1585. As for the northward-trekking Lost Colony, the only firm statement came years later from the emperor Powhatan, who claimed to have "bin at the murther of that Colonie: and shewed to Captain Smith a Musket barrell and a brasse Morter, and certain peeces of Iron which had bin theirs."[81]

How soon after that the colonists moved out remains anybody's guess, but Powhatan's claim is clear evidence that some (probably most) went sufficiently far northward to fall into the net of his chieftaincy.[82] A clue used to provide a *terminus ante quem* for their departure comes from a Spanish source. In June 1588, while returning to Havana from seeking the "Cittie of Ralegh" in the Chesapeake, Captain Vicente González stopped at the North Carolina Outer Banks and "on the inside of a little bay, came upon a slipway for small vessels, and on land a number of wells made with English casks, and other debris indicating that a considerable number of people had been here."[83] That statement has been used to contend that the Spaniards had landed on Roanoke Island and found the settlers gone. That they could have been so myopic as to peer down wells and see that their linings were constructed from English barrels while failing to notice the "very fort-like palisades" that should have encompassed them makes no sense. More reasonable is the alternative that the little bay was on the sound side of the Outer Banks and that what Gonzales saw was a developed location akin to the one to which Lane sent Captain Stafford and his twenty men in 1586.

Chapter 2

FORT RALEIGH

The Later History

The location at the north end of Roanoke Island that John White described as "by the water side, round about the North point of the island," and where he said he "left our Colony in the yeere 1586," reputedly is the location of the archaeological site known to the National Park Service as Fort Raleigh.[84] The island still has a northerly projection around which one can walk (as did White) to reach it. Simple logic, therefore, would seem to dictate that the place where Elizabethan artifacts have been found is the site of the palisaded settlement visited by White in 1590 and which, by extension, had to have been the place briefly inhabited by Grenville's tiny garrison and previously constructed by Ralph Lane's settlers in September 1585. This reasoning, however, does not take into consideration the rate of erosion at the island's northerly extremity and the question of whether what was by the water in 1590 could be far out in it four centuries later.

Writing in 1960, archaeologist Jean C. Harrington summarized the then available erosion-rate data and concluded that the loss "at the north point…a half mile west of the fort, has been around 700 feet during the past 140 years, and that erosion opposite the fort [had] been in the neighborhood of 200 feet during the same period." Harrington warned, however, that it would be unwise to assume that the rate had been continuous since 1585. On the contrary, he noted, most of it may have occurred after 1820.[85]

Although the testimony of other early colonial sites suggests that settlements usually were located at the water's edge so as to provide (a) a means of escape if attacked from the land and (b) an opportunity to prevent a waterborne enemy from landing, there is no evidence to say that Ralph Lane's village was constructed at the waterside. On the contrary, the time that Grenville's men took to fight their way to their boat and the distance that John White had to walk back to the settlement from the "Creeke" suggest that it was not. However, being removed from the water's edge in 1590 and still being on dry land in the 1990s are not necessarily the same. If, therefore, and as will be demonstrated, there was more than one 1585–88 occupation site, one of them further inland than the other, there is no guarantee that each early island explorer saw the same remains.

In spite of several attempts to seek out the Lost Colonists either alive or dead—first by Raleigh in 1602 and, later, after the Virginia Company had settled on Jamestown Island—nothing substantive was learned. In 1653, however, a fur trader visited Roanoke Island and was shown the remains of "Sir Walter Raleigh's fort" and brought away a now-unidentified "sure token of their being there."[86]

Half a century later, the previously cited John Lawson was there and recalled that "the Ruins of a Fort are to be seen at this day." In addition to the quarterdeck gun, he noted that English coins had been found, along with a brass gun and a powder horn.[87] By the turn of the eighteenth century, therefore, the site was a recognized historic place of interest to travelers, few and far between as they were. Twenty-eight years later, however, the earliest detailed plat of the island (copying a survey of 1718) failed to mark it, as did the survey. Indeed, it would not be until 1770 that a fort would appear on a published map, albeit somewhat to the east of the island's northern tip. This,

Silver sixpence (obverse and reverse) of Elizabeth I dated 1563 and pierced for suspension above the queen's crown. Found near the Fort Raleigh National Historic Site, the coin is believed to have been given to an Indian as a portrait of the new ruler over the ocean. *FCF.*

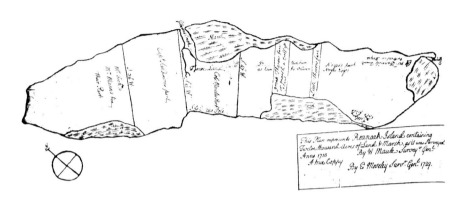

A plat of Roanoke Island first drawn in 1718 by W. Maule and redrawn in 1729 by E. Moseley to suit his patrons. Shallowbag Bay is here shown almost entirely marsh filled. Some have argued that the Raleigh era settlements were located where Gibson's Creek flanks Baum Point. *Cumming 1998 No. 203, presently part of the Hayes Collection at Southern Historical Collection, Wilson Library, UNC.*

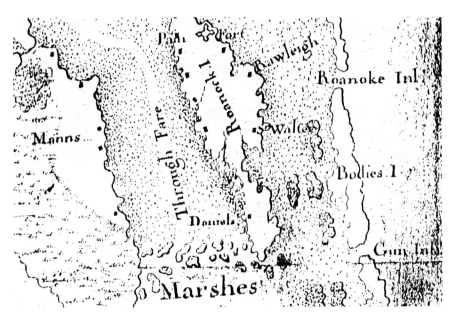

Detail from John Collet's original 1768 map of North Carolina showing Roanoke Island and his use of Sir Walter Raleigh's name apparently in connection with the fort word and symbol above. *Cumming 1998 No. 362. Original: British Library, King George III Topographical Collection, cxxii.52.2 Table.*

the John Collet map of North Carolina, was based on an original drawing of 1768 and included many minor changes wrought by the engraver.

The words *Fort*, *Raleigh* and *Walter* burined in different lettering, one above the other, in the sound east of the island have been variously interpreted. Most scholars are of the opinion that all relate to the drawn fort: Sir Walter Raleigh's Fort. However, one might equally interpret the wordings' placement as suggesting that the 1585–88 settlement had been located somewhere between "Sr. Walter" and "Rawleigh." On the 1770 map, the name Pain occurs on the west side of the island at its north end, and it is known that on June 2, 1767, John Paine paid one John Mann twenty pounds for fifty acres at that end of the island. In 1775, however, the Collet map was reengraved, this time attributed to "Henry Mouzon and Others." Not knowing the Paine connection, the copier shifted that name to the east and provided a new identification for the square and flankered fort symbol: "Pain Fort." The Mouzon map also showed a shipping channel to Edenton passing close to the north end of the island, suggesting—if one did not think one knew better—that the fort was a contemporary structure erected either to protect the island from a seaborne invader or to fire on enemy shipping passing through Roanoke Inlet. Although the map shows a sizeable vessel doing just that, as early as circa 1700, when Lawson made his survey, he observed that Roanoke Inlet was too shallow for the passage of anything larger than a sloop or a brigantine.

Assuming that, on his map, John Collet meant to show the Roanoke fort symbol as a historic site, it differs not at all from other fort symbols on his maps of the Carolinas, at least one of which calls an abandoned fort an "old fort." That historic sites were of sufficient interest to merit inclusion on eighteenth-century maps is demonstrated by those showing the site of the 1607 Popham Colony's Fort St. George in Maine. The first, dating from 1731, identifies the settlement by name; the next, of 1751, calls it "old fort," while the United States Geological Survey of 1868 went further and identified the location as that of Ancient Ft. George.[88] Be that as it was, no surviving charts or maps of Roanoke Island in the nineteenth century show any historic site at its north end. That is not to say, however, that nobody remembered Ralph Lane's "Newe Forte" or that nobody cared.

In 1819, President Monroe made a tour of the southern coastline to inspect potential defensible sites, and in so doing, stopped in Albemarle Sound to discuss the possibility of opening a new inlet to admit larger shipping to Edenton. While there, he was taken to Roanoke Island to "view the remains of the Fort, the traces of which are still distinctly visible, which is said to have

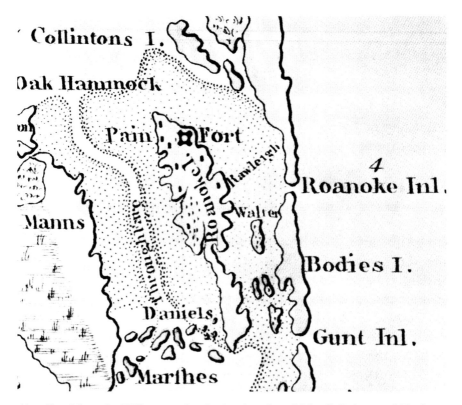

Above: Detail from the 1770 engraved and printed version of John Collet's map of North Carolina showing the revised rendering of Roanoke Island and the related (comp. Collett map on page 56). *Cumming 1998 No. 394.*

Opposite: Detail from Henry Mouzon's 1775 re-engraving of the 1770 printing of John Collet's map, showing the name PAIN in immediate juxtaposition to the word FORT. The only noticeable differences with Collet around Roanoke Island seem to be Mouzon's use of the channel soundings from Wimble map from 1730s. *Cumming 1998 No. 450.*

been erected by the first colony of Sir Walter Raleigh."[89] What, one may wonder, was the president shown? Was it the same "ruin" that Lawson had seen in 1701 and where he had found military artifacts, or had time, wind and tide already claimed that for the sea?

Whatever it was, the site was not of sufficient prominence to merit inclusion in engineer Hamilton Fulton's 1820 map of the island's flanking sounds. For him, it was enough to inscribe "Dough" at the approximate fort location, that being the name of a family prominent on the island then and now. One might conclude, therefore, that the previous year's enthusiasm for history that had sparked a presidential visit quickly waned when life got back

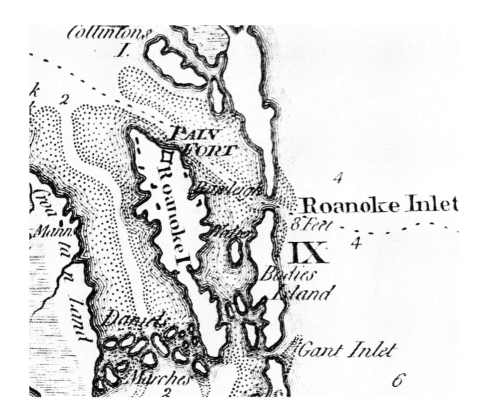

to normal. Nevertheless, anyone visiting the island who remembered their history books knew that this was where the Lost Colony got lost, and with little else to do, a trip to "the place where" could lead to a few vicariously exciting hours. Among the pilgrims was the celebrated artist Benson J. Lossing, who apparently knew more about the site's history than most tourists do today. After a visit in 1849, he wrote that "slight traces of Lane's fort" were to be seen at the island's north end.[90] There is, of course, no knowing how slight were the slight traces. In the same year, however, another visitor to the site had something much more definitive to report. George Higby Throop would write that at "the remains of the fort, glass globes, containing quicksilver, and hermetically sealed and other relics occasionally discovered there, give rise to a thousand conjectures destined never to be solved."[91]

Whereas Lawson's fort contained military artifacts, Throop's yielded glass balls of mercury, a substance used by metallurgical assayers. Agricola (Bauer) described the use of mercury in the recovery of gold in his *De Re Metallica*. Furthermore, early engravings and woodcuts of assayers' tools and activities include tongs for enclosing distillates and other materials

This is a furnice for the closeing of the mouths or necks of glass bottles together. It is made all of Iron cast with an hole in the side and set in an Iron Brandrat: and reaching aboue the furnice top set a strong paire of Tongs with broad ends, so that the neck of the glass being made hot, with the glowing tongs it is wringed or squeesed together, and so closely vnited as if it were whole.

An illustration from Randle Holme's *Academy of Armory* (1682) showing the furnace and tongs used to seal the necks of phials of glass globes. *Public domain.*

in sealed-mouth glass vials.[92] There can be no doubt that Throop was reporting the discovery of valuable material left behind by Joachim Gans when he and all his fellows abruptly abandoned their homes and workplaces in June 1586. One may fairly ask, therefore, whether mere chance governed the disparate discoveries reported by Lawson and Throop or whether, perhaps, each had visited different "forts," one for the protection of people and the other for the products of research. If true, then Lane's inference that Thomas Harriot's house stood sufficiently apart from the rest to necessitate attack by a different force of Indians gains credence. The flaw in that reasoning, of course, is that nobody ever mentioned there being two forts at any one time.

Assuming, if only as a debating point, that Harriot's workplace and house were located within a fort, what kind of fort did the nineteenth-century visitors think it to have been?[93]

Writing for *Harper's New Monthly Magazine* in May 1860, Edward C. Bruce insisted that the site of "Master Ralph Layne's [*sic*] stronghold and the City of Raleigh" was well known and that "every body on the island is familiar with it....The intrenchments speak a mute testimony of their own....The trench is clearly traceable in a square of about forty yards each way....The ditch is generally two feet deep, though in many places scarcely perceptible. The whole site," Bruce added, "is overgrown with pine, live oak, vines, and a variety of other plants, high and low."[94]

Two years later, describing a much earlier visit to the site, New Hampshire resident Frederic Kidder remembered that the remains of Lane's fort were "very slight, being merely the wreck of an embankment. This," he went on, "has at times been excavated by parties who hoped to find some deposit which would repay the trouble, but with little success, a vial of quicksilver being the only relic said to have been found."[95]

A detachment of the Ninth New York (Hawkin's Zouaves) storming a Confederate artillery earthwork on Roanoke Island. *Drawn by an* Illustrated London News *war artist for the March 22, 1862 issue.*

February 1862 found Roanoke Island at war, with Union troops under General Ambrose Burnside driving the Confederates from one hastily constructed earthwork to another. With resistance quelled, the Union troops camped at the north end of the island at a location west of the historic fort site that was in easy reach of Yankee treasure hunters. More holes were dug into the fragile remains, and they yielded a still surviving axe-head.[96] Landowner Walter Dough persuaded Union officers to declare the site off-limits and to place it under military guard—but after "holes were dug into the embankment at the eastern angle and on the southeastern face."[97]

In mid-July 1862, one of those bored soldiers, Charles F. Johnson of Colonel Hawkins's Zouaves, described what he saw when he visited the site to draw the "Earth-work built by Sir Walter Raleigh's Colony." He provided the only known rendering of the remains as they were in the mid-nineteenth century. A more than averagely educated soldier, Johnson concluded that the site was not all it claimed to be:

> *For my part, I don't think Sir Walter had anything to do with the Fort; but if you will refer to the History of the United States, you will find that*

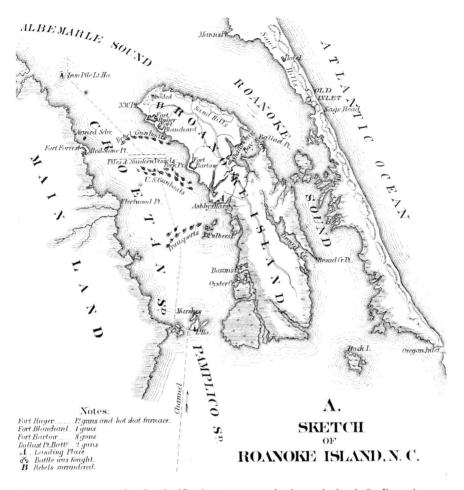

A contemporary map showing fortifications constructed prior to the battle for Roanoke Island and marking sand hills and wooded land along the island's north shore. U.S. major general J.G. Foster submitted this 1862 map to the Committee on the Conduct of the Warr to document the Battle of Roanoke Island. *Library of Congress, online.*

there was a colony, or a nucleus of one, of fifteen or twenty men left on the island, of which nothing was ever heard afterward.... They were probably butchered by Indians, and that this fort had something to do with them—in fact, it was thrown up for their defense against the Indians—I have no doubt in my mind.

Johnson went on to state that stone and flint arrowheads had been found on the site, and those, in his view, were proof that "red and white men's blood mingled over this spot in the lonely woods." He was not impressed

Left: An iron axe-head found by Union soldiers digging at the Fort Raleigh site in 1862. *Walter Raleigh Collection of the University of North Carolina.*

Below: Zouave Charles Johnson's 1862 drawing of the Fort Raleigh earthwork. From his 1911 book *The Long Roll*.

Earthwork; Built by Sir Walter Raleigh's Colony, Roanoke Island

by the fort's physical remains, noting that "the breastworks are not more than ordinary mounds now, and anyone who was not shown the place would probably pass over it a hundred times without discovering anything so unusual as to warrant the thought of a fortification." However, without Johnson's text, his pencil sketch could be interpreted as a well-preserved embankment rising several feet in its flat-topped height, albeit overgrown with trees and shrubs.[98]

Thirty-seven years later, a lifelong island resident, R. Bruce Etheridge, expressed surprise that the sand-constructed *low mound, scarcely higher than a grave had managed to survive through so many centuries. It is only little short of a miracle of accidents that this crumbling mound "Child of silence and slow time" has escaped destruction. The elements have spared it on an Island where the merest exposure of the loose, thin soil starts shifting sands to pile dunes and level them.*[99]

Etheridge has not been alone in expressing surprise that a sand-constructed earthwork should survive for so long, and while in the more innocent Victorian age, miracles may have been more frequent than they are today, other explanations cannot be ruled out.

Etheridge, in his zeal to promote the site as a state and national treasure, contended that not only had it been spared the detrition of time or plow, but it had also escaped "the ravages of the relic hunter." However, the amateur archaeologist Talcott Williams, who was destined to play as major a role as any in exploring the past while ensuring a future for the Fort Raleigh site, was less sanguine. "I strongly urge fencing the site at once," he declared. "It is being visited, caves cut & trees marked after our mad American fashion." Williams voiced this concern in late 1895, while on the island to undertake the site's first archaeological investigation.[100]

Beginning around 1890, local worthies, Etheridge among them, began to agitate toward the creation of a formal association to protect and to promote their historic site—the promotion focusing on the forthcoming Columbian Exposition at Chicago in 1893. To this end, a largely distaff group created the Virginia Dare Columbian Memorial Association. However, the male-dominated committee for North Carolina's contributions to the World's Columbian Exhibition failed to be as supportive as had been hoped. Virginia Dare failed to get the recognition the ladies had hoped for, and in 1894, their association had faded and was replaced by the Roanoke Colony Memorial Association, which in 1894 purchased a 250-acre tract that took in the by then well-known historic site. The new association's secretary-treasurer, John S. Bassett, felt that archaeological verification should now take precedence over legend and conjecture, and it was he who contacted Talcott Williams. The latter's prior archaeological experience is not known, but he was then serving on the board of the Archaeological Museum of the University of Pennsylvania.

The 1890s were a period of considerable archaeological activity in Greece, Egypt, Mesopotamia and Central America, and in England, retired general Pitt Rivers was developing at Cranborne Chase a methodology for

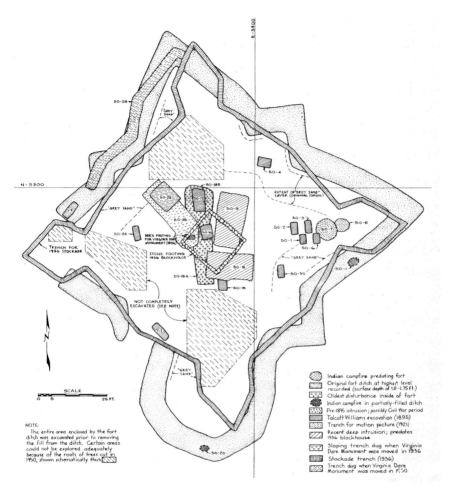

J.C. Harrington's plan of the Roanoke Island earthwork site locating the features of different dates that had disturbed both the ditch and the fort's interior, as well as the hatched areas not explored in 1950 prior to the structure's reconstruction.

archaeological excavation that was new to everyone (with the exception of the late Thomas Jefferson). Rather than randomly digging hither and yon, he "substituted the total excavation of sites." Pitt Rivers "stressed the importance of stratigraphical observation, and of the necessity of recording the position of everything found. He caused accurate plans and sections and detailed drawings and descriptions to be made of all his excavations, and constructed models of all the main sites."[101] Because Pitt Rivers is considered to have been so far ahead of his time, and because American archaeological practices would take a long time to parallel his work, Talcott

Williams's account of his test excavations on Roanoke Island is deserving of more credit than it has been allowed. It reads in part:

> *The site of each trench was carefully plotted and fixed by bearings and measurements, and a minute record kept and deposited with the association, so that no injury would be done to the site and no embarrassment caused to any future explorer by his inability to know where the soil was disturbed. In all, 13 trenches, most of them 5 by 3 feet were opened and carried from 4 to 9 feet deep.*[102] *Water, it may be premised, is reached at 15 feet, and undisturbed sand at about 4 feet. Wherever trenches were sunk, and it is fair to conclude, over the entire area, there was found a thin and undisturbed layer of sandy humus of 6 to 8 inches to a foot, then a layer of black, ashy earth, containing many fragments of charcoal and frequent fire pits.*[103] *This layer rested directly on undisturbed sand, often penetrated by fire pits. If we imagine a forest surface from which the original humus had been removed to make an embankment, laying bare the sand below, this site occupied for a season and then for three centuries left to gather humus again, the condition revealed would be created. Toward the base of the black, ashy layer were found small pieces of iron, a corroded nail, a chipped piece of quartzite, and small fragments of Indian pottery, networked.*[104]

Williams's description of the Fort Raleigh site's stratigraphy is both clear and accurate. It is evident that he examined every artifact, however small, with great care and recorded its placement in the way that General Pitt Rivers prescribed. It is possible, however, that Williams's "small pieces of iron" may have been natural bog iron conglomerates, many of which were found in later excavations and initially confused with heavily encrusted nail fragments. Still discussing his artifacts, Williams went on to observe that "no one could reasonably expect to find any objects of importance on a site ransacked as this must have been, but I confess my surprise," he added, at the absence of small fragments, "particularly of pottery. For a site occupied as it was, the place proved singularly barren of debris. Like [the fort's] size, this circumstance has no ready explanation."[105]

Talcott Williams's excavation test pits or trenches were largely confined to the interior of the earthwork, and of the twelve later encountered by archaeologist Harrington, only one extended outward to the silted ditch. Thus, his observations regarding the dearth of artifacts were based on the assumption that the fort's interior had been intensively and domestically occupied. Had that been the case, Williams's surprise would have been fully justified, although his acceptance of Indian looting as a cause for the artifacts' absence is easily countered. John White's description of his breeched chests, for example, makes it clear that the Indians only took things that they liked or considered useful and that they were not above damaging objects (like books) and taking away only those pieces that appealed to them. That they did not include White's plate armor among the desirable loot leaves little doubt that much would have remained after the village had been invaded. Then, too, one must consider that the products of clumsiness, coupled with domestic waste and refuse, account for nine-tenths of all artifacts found on domestic sites. With more than 100 residents housed there for the best part of a year before departing in precipitous haste, to be followed by 15 more whose stores were burned and finally succeeded by close to 120 of White's men, women and children, broken artifacts and food waste should be present in large quantities. Indeed, the absence of animal, fish and bird bones, as well as of oyster and clam shells, should have told Williams that if anyone lived inside the fort, they almost certainly cooked and dined elsewhere.

Although Talcott Williams (like every other archaeologist) was disappointed not to find some amazing and unequivocally diagnostic artifact, he could

Members of the Roanoke Colony Memorial Association earning photographic immortality alongside their 1896 tribute to Virginia Dare. *NPS.*

confidently report to his sponsor John Bassett that having found small pieces of iron at a depth of twenty-one inches "below an undisturbed surface they prove European occupation at the date when the fort was erected."[106]

That was the news that the Roanoke Colony Memorial Association needed to go forward. Small concrete markers were then seated at each corner of the earthwork's outline, and an inscribed granite monument was set up inside the fort in 1896. The association's struggle to remain solvent through the next twenty years has no bearing on the site itself and so is irrelevant. Suffice it to say that the enthusiasm of the 1890s faded, and with motorized tourism still in its infancy, the site was used more by local picnickers than by Anglophilic pilgrims.

Fort Raleigh received an important (but ground-scarring) boost in 1921 when the Atlas Film Corporation of Chicago, sponsored by the North Carolina Board of Education, arrived to make a five-reel silent film, none too imaginatively titled *The Lost Colony*. Unfortunately, rather than filming on the neighboring dunes, the director chose to increase authenticity by erecting her set on the very place trodden by the soon-to-be-lost colonists. The result was a seventy-foot-long trench slicing into the old fort's silted ditch that did serious damage to the entire west side.

Further and even more serious damage would occur in 1924 when an old live oak that stood in the center of the enclosed area was deliberately knocked over. Regardless of the fact that the site was defined both by markers and the monument, the State Highway Commission's workers cut through the site to create an automobile turnaround at the end of a dirt road. The road builders reportedly claimed to have had no idea that they were on the historic site. "In the meantime," added the newspaper report, "the September rains washed the unprotected soil, and the joy riding public is cutting deep furrows in a spot that should be hallowed by the nation."[107] The local citizenry was reported to be "hurt, but passive and powerless." But worse was yet to come, and the historic site's mentors had no one to blame but themselves.

By 1931, the Roanoke Colony Memorial Association was aging and ready to let a new organization continue to lead the charge. It emerged in the shape of a freshly created Roanoke Island Historical Association. Together, they laid plans for a grand 350th anniversary celebrating the landing of Captains Amadas and Barlowe in 1584. But the nation was in the midst of the Great Depression, and no state money was available to underwrite what the Carolinian needy might have regarded as historical frivolity. So rather than abandon the celebration, it was postponed until 1937—to coincide with the birth of Virginia Dare and the arrival of the last colonists.

The earthwork site outlined by small concrete and intermediate wooden posts with the Virginia Dare marker in the middle, photographed prior to the erection of the palisade and blockhouse in 1936. *NPS.*

The Depression had its benefits, not the least of them the provision of Civilian Conservation Corpsmen (CCC) to improve national and state parks—usually by building from logs—virtually anything that would stand up. With that free labor seeking employment, North Carolina's governor, J.C.B. Ehringhaus, set up a commission of three men (E. Bruce Etheridge being one of them) to design and supervise the construction on and around the Fort Raleigh site of the kind of log blockhouse, church, museum, houses, restrooms and ticket booth that the Lost Colony would have occupied and needed. Perhaps in recognition of the rebuilding of eighteenth-century Williamsburg in Virginia, the Fort Raleigh "improvements," too, were defined as a restoration. The 1932 charter of the Roanoke Island Historical Association made no bones about its commitment to such a project, the

Settlement at Roanoke.

A mid-nineteenth-century American history textbook depiction of the Roanoke settlement as a collection of log cabins and thus precedent for the 1936 reconstruction. *Public domain.*

association's mandate empowering it "to establish and maintain one or more areas or sites for the permanent location of buildings and other structures, with convenient facilities, for preserving the historical background and representing the settlement and habits of life of the early colonists."[108] It is true that the charter said nothing about building log cabins, but it also is true that as early as 1851, engravings of Fort Raleigh's purported log-cabined village had been published in American history books.[109]

The bulk of the Fort Raleigh "restorations" were erected on land adjacent to the historic earthwork's traces, although by the laying of water and electrical lines, damage was done to areas not then known to be sensitive. It was, however, the fort itself that suffered most. Ignoring the evidential traces of the silted ditch, a tree-pole palisade was erected to create a square stockade with projecting, arrow-shaped flankers at each corner. Inside it, a log blockhouse was built in a style reminiscent of nineteenth-century

The frontier fort–style blockhouse erected in 1936 inside the timber palisade atop the site's earthwork remains. *NPS.*

The earthwork outlined in cement slabs after parts of the palisade blew down in 1944. Posts in the foreground flank the paved road that overlay the 1965–93 discoveries. *NPS.*

frontier forts and of National Park Service support buildings. Seated on a cobblestone foundation, this anomalous structure overlay two large pits that postdated Talcott Williams's trenches and sat atop the brick foundation for the 1896 Virginia Dare monument (see the map on page 65). By the time this work of "restoration" was completed, all visible traces of the ditched fort seen by President Monroe and by other nineteenth-century visitors had been obscured.

The Roanoke Island Historical Association's contributions to the authenticity of the site were not sustained. To take advantage of the improvements that could be made through federal CCC help, the Roanoke Colony Memorial Association deeded the historic site to the State of North Carolina in 1934, which transferred it to the federal government and thus to the U.S. National Park Service in 1939. Well aware that the 1934 state commission's research had been less than thorough, Park Service historians were undismayed when a 1944 hurricane caused sections of the fort's stockade to be "razed down." Such poles as were still erect were cut off at ground level—inadvertently creating a future archaeological feature of no little significance. With the palisade gone, the fort was next outlined by rectangular cement blocks laid like fallen dominoes to follow the previously determined, but always conjectural, enclosure plan.

The end of the Second World War provided the impetus to put the Fort Raleigh National Historic Site in a fit shape to receive its post-victory visitors, and to that end, Jamestown's and the region's National Park Service archaeologist Jean C. Pinky Harrington was brought down in 1947 to excavate the fort's remains more thoroughly than had Talcott Williams and to provide new recommendation as to how it might be authentically reconstructed. Thus began the archaeological phase of the site's history.

Chapter 3

FORT RALEIGH

The Archaeology, 1947–85

The arrival of Dr. J.C. "Pinky" Harrington marked the commencement of an entirely new approach to the study of the Fort Raleigh site. Like the Roanoke restoration, Harrington as an archaeologist was a product of the Depression. He had trained as an architect and intended to remain one, until the head of his firm jumped from an office window, resulting not only in his own demise but also that of his company. Unemployed, Harrington enrolled at the University of Chicago and there obtained a PhD in anthropology. During this period, excavations had been in progress on the National Park Service's newly acquired acres at Jamestown—one of America's earliest ventures into what is now called historical archaeology.[110] Guidance and, indeed, the senior personnel came from the laid-off staff of Colonial Williamsburg, which closed down its excavations in 1933. Draftsmen who had supervised the digging in Williamsburg gravitated to the Park Service and to its excavations on the Yorktown Battlefield and thence to Jamestown. Consequently, the experience of these neo-archaeologists related primarily to eighteenth-century brick foundations, features easily discovered with picks and shovels. Although Jamestown's later buildings yielded comparable remains, the earlier structures, being post-set and with interrupted wooden sills that left nothing but dirty marks in the ground, were not to be found by those methods. Furthermore, the Williamsburg excavators knew nothing about the dating of domestic artifacts but only about those that related to buildings: hinges, locks, window glass, nails, etc.[111]

One of J.C. Harrington's 1947 trenches showing in the foreground the stubs of juniper post remaining from the 1936 palisade. *NPS.*

When it became known that Jamestown was being excavated by architects having no anthropological background, the Park Service was under pressure to rectify the problem. It did so by appointing anthropologists to the project. But the architects and anthropologists did not gel: the former complained that the anthropologists knew nothing about colonial foundations, while the latter contended that the architects, through their lack of broad cultural knowledge and of archaeological field training, were butchering the site.[112] In 1936, unable to keep the peace, an exasperated Park Service disposed of both and sought a single replacement who possessed both architectural and anthropological credentials. In those early days, seeking such an individual was like searching the proverbial haystack, but the needle existed in the person of Pinky Harrington.

Harrington would later confess that after accepting the appointment, he had no idea where Jamestown was located or what to expect when he got there. Nevertheless, helped by conservator Worth Bailey, he was quickly able to get the project onto firm ground, and through the years leading up to the Second World War, he developed techniques and avenues of artifactual research that earned him his place as the father of modern historical archaeology in America. Consequently, it was inevitable that when the Park Service needed an archaeologist to excavate Jamestown's immediate predecessor, Harrington would be the obvious choice. Nevertheless, as he had on arriving at Jamestown, he found himself in uncharted waters. With the 1607 fort at Jamestown presumed to have been lost to river erosion, he had had no prior experience of excavating the mutilated remains of an earthwork, nor had he any refined knowledge of Elizabethan artifacts.[113] Furthermore, he would find his options severely limited by Park Service instructions not to damage or remove trees. "I was dodging between trees and around paved roads and surfaced trails still in use," he wrote.[114]

In 1946 and in his capacity as the Park Service's regional archaeologist, Harrington laid out a preliminary program for archaeology at Fort Raleigh. Writing with characteristic caution, he stated, "The available evidence is fairly conclusive that the traditional Fort site is the site of the original Fort Raleigh, although this cannot be demonstrated with absolute certainty."[115] In the following year and continuing in 1948, Harrington conducted trenching excavations that straddled the fort ditch and explored in several, largely westerly, directions beyond it. At this operation's conclusion, he felt sufficiently confident to make the determination that warranted the earthwork's reconstruction:

> *The two seasons' explorations at Fort Raleigh National Historic Site have shown, beyond reasonable doubt, that the site is that of the Raleigh settlements on Roanoke Island. They have established the identity, type of construction, and plan of Ralph Lane's fort, built there in 1585. They*

failed to locate the site of the village, which was presumably in the general vicinity of the fort, but they did reveal certain conditions which strongly suggest that the settlement may have been located in the area immediately west of the fort.[116]

Based on the success of his 1947–48 investigations, Harrington was able to plan more extensive excavations that led, in 1950 and 1951, to the dirt fort's reconstruction. During that time, he was able to excavate most of the undisturbed ditch and fort interior and to carefully plot the placement of each artifact. Within the ditched enclosure, he also found the remains of the earthwork overlying the sixteenth-century land surface and sealing under it several unquestionably early European artifacts, the most dateably recognizable among them being part of an Iberian earthenware jar. But the most important would be a lump of worked copper waste.

Harrington reported that the ditch varied from three to four feet in depth and was from two to three feet wide at the bottom.

The nature of the fill revealed quite clearly that the initial filling of the ditch occurred very soon after the fort was constructed, since the bottom few inches was clean sand, with no humus accumulation whatever at the bottom....Higher in the ditch, however, irregular accumulations of humus were encountered, indicating a gradual filling over the years, but with occasional rapid deposits, presumably from erosion of the parapet.[117]

Most of the artifacts recovered from the fort area came not from its interior but from the several layers of the ditch fill. Among them was a second lump of cuprous waste similar to that noted earlier. Together they presented a depositional problem, one lump being deposited on the land surface *before* the earthwork was erected and the other finding its way into the ditch long *after* it had been abandoned.[118] Raising unanswered questions, too, was the discovery of an apothecary's nested weight only one foot from the top of the four-foot silted ditch.[119] Why, one might have wondered, did this Elizabethan-style object wait so long to reach its resting place?[120]

Unquestionably of sixteenth- or early seventeenth-century date were two copper alloy casting counters (also known as jettons) for calculations on a checkered board or cloth. These two had been made by a Hans Schultes of Nuremberg, one of three jetton makers of that name, the last of whom is undocumented after 1612.[121] Although found at the fort site, neither is from a stratified early context. They are paralleled by another Schultes jetton

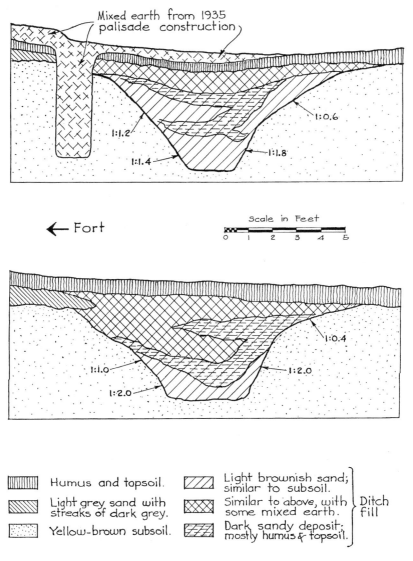

Sections through the earthwork's ditch as revealed by J.C. Harrington in 1948. *NPS.*

found at Buxton on the Outer Banks, suggesting that this last is a relic of trade with the Croatoan Indians.[122] No less "of the period" are fragments from a polychrome-decorated, tin-enameled *albarillo* (ointment pot) made either in the Netherlands or perhaps in Norwich, England (see the drawing on page 136). Alas, these sherds are among those for which no pertinent dating context exists.

Top: A lump of worked copper from the earthwork's ditch filling (no. 87). *Photo by Ira Block.*

Middle: In the foreground an apothecary's weight (23.5 x 10 mm, FORA 40) found one foot below the top of the filled ditch, shown with a comparable set of nested brass weights (FORA 48-56). *Photo by Ira Block.*

Bottom: The Spanish jar neck found by J.C. Harrington at the bottom of the earthwork's ditch (no. 81). *Photo by Ira Block.*

Opposite: The earthwork and the moved Virginia Dare monument photographed shortly after the reconstruction was complete, but not before the protecting turfs had begun to slide downward. *NPS.*

The fort's reconstruction was eventually completed and covered with turf to protect it from the ravages of rain, for as R. Bruce Etheridge had noted, "the merest exposure of the loose, thin soil starts shifting sand to pile dunes and level them."[123] A photograph taken soon after the reconstruction was complete shows what appear to be dislodged turfs sliding haphazardly down into the ditch.

Although the height of the rampart or berm was carefully calculated on the basis of the soil and sandy clay displaced by digging the ditch, and regardless of the fact that the ditch outline was meticulously followed, the relatively soft contours of the end product were more attuned to the needs of artillery than of musketeers—unless they were prepared to expose themselves to enemy fire. In discussing steps he would like to have taken had Grenville's supplies arrived in April 1586, Ralph Lane described how he would have "raised a sconse with a small trench, and a pallisado upon the top of it, in the which, and in the guard of my boates I would have left five and twenty, or thirty men." He went on to speak of building another to hold fifteen or twenty, adding that he would hope to have "raised my saide sconse upon some Corne fielde, that my company might have lived upon it."[124] The significant factor here is that Lane would have topped his earthwork with a wooden breastwork palisade over which, and from behind which, his musketeers could fire. But there being no trace of posts in the ground of Fort Raleigh, attention to the burden of proof dictated that this all-important defensive element should be omitted. In truth, of course, unless the posts went four or more feet down through the rampart, they would not have penetrated the old land surface and would have left no postholes. Without such a breastwork enabling defenders to stand atop the rampart, as noted above, the structure is better suited to artillery, whose servitors and gunners would remain behind the earthen rampart. Although it must be allowed that John White's rendering of the sandcastle fortifications on the Puerto Rican beach shows no such palisaded breastwork, one may counter that from the scale of the people inside it, the rampart itself was no higher than a breastwork—though how it stayed together with a water-filled ditch beyond it stretches credulity.

The earthwork reconstructed, ca. 1951. Note the post and rail edging to the roadway (*right, background*) and (*left*) a sample panel of breastwork palisade. *NPS.*

The possibility that the Fort Raleigh earthwork had been topped with a chest-high palisade has been used by some to explain why Pedro Diaz referred to Lane's defenses as being no more than a wooden fort of little strength. It may be no coincidence, however, that the reconstructed earthwork is of a size far better suited to protect the fifteen or twenty whom Lane proposed to leave in his smaller sconce than to provide a bawn-like refuge for more than one hundred retreating colonists. Be that as it may, the record shows that Ralph Lane had in mind the building of earth and palisaded fortlets. In the absence of later-to-be-discovered conflicting evidence, it remained a possibility that the Fort Raleigh site was really that of one such distant defense work and that the village had yet to be found elsewhere.

Harrington addressed this possibility in his 1962 report but did not give it much credence:

> If, for the moment, we consider the traditional fort as an outlying sconce, the second, and even more pertinent, question is where the main fort and settlement might have been located....If we did not have a perfectly good fort of approximately the right date at the northwest end of the island, and had to rely entirely on historical records, we would undoubtedly place the settlement and fort in the general vicinity of Mother's Vineyard....Certainly such a proposal could never be accepted unless the remains of a larger fort, preferably in association with a palisaded enclosure, were found through archaeological explorations, or unless new documentary evidence turns up.[125]

Had one enjoyed the luxury of hindsight in the 1960s, one might have asked: but what if you don't have a perfectly good fort, and it turns out not to be of approximately the right date and visitors continue to think it too small to protect so many colonists—what then?

In ending his landmark report (still one of the most readable and informative contributions to historical archaeology yet published), Harrington discussed the need for further archaeology at the Fort Raleigh site:

> Tradition and a perfectly good archaeological relic notwithstanding, it would seem indefensible at this point to state without qualification that the original settlement was west of the excavated fort. Even less defensible would be the expenditure of a large sum to excavate too far in this general direction in search of the elusive townsite....Even so, some additional exploration in the vicinity of the fort is called for, and clearly warranted.[126]

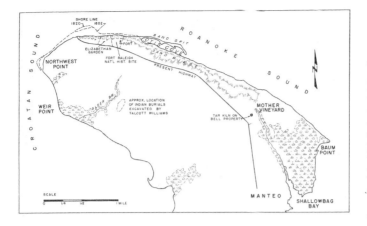

The north end of Roanoke Island showing Fort Raleigh and the competing Mother Vineyard location. *Map from Harrington's 1962 report. Public domain.*

It often happens in the field of historic preservation that once the ribbon has been cut, eagerness to do more rapidly wanes. Although the colonists' village had not been found, and although many visitors came to the site expecting to see it, the Department of the Interior saw the Fort Raleigh National Historic Site as a completed historic area rather than as a continuing research project. There was no enthusiasm for more digging.

But in 1959, while laying a waterline to a drinking fountain inside the reconstructed fort, a patch of burned clay or underfired brick fragments was uncovered—and the waterline was relocated to avoid it. The patch lay under a roadway that looped around the park immediately west of the fort, an area not previously explored. Five years later, when the Park Service was making major visitor-friendly improvements that included removing the road as well as the last of the major 1936 log cabins, Harrington was called back to investigate the 1959 discovery. A plethora of undesirable circumstances prevented him from undertaking a single, methodical excavation of all of the potentially pertinent area. Instead, helped only by his archaeologist wife, Virginia, and a crew of one to three Park employees, the excavation was undertaken in four bites in February, March, May and October. Nevertheless, the Harringtons' discoveries were to turn conventional wisdom on its ear.

The area of brick that had been thought might be a walkway or even the laid bib to a hearth turned out to be brickbat rubble in the filling of a rectangular pit, itself within the sandy fill of another circular pit. The discovery of Indian potsherds amid the brickbats initially suggested that the feature was an aboriginal firepit and evidence that Indians had cooked on the site after brick-laid structures erected by the colonists had been torn down.

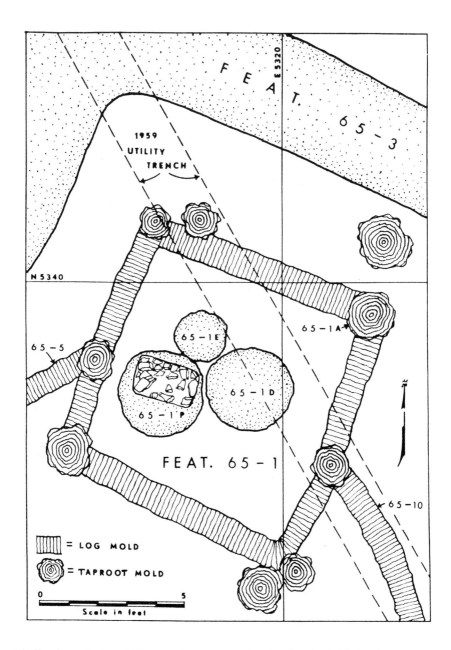

J.C. Harrington's plan of his outwork structure and its interior pits. *Public domain.*

During the second phase of his four-stage excavation, Harrington removed the brickbats and noted that they "did not appear to be set, but we are finding pieces of hard, flat clay 1/2" thick, that look like 'mortar.'" There is little doubt that Harrington was right and that the structure of which the bricks had been part had been mortared with puddled clay. Strewn around the pits as well as in their fill were considerable quantities of charcoal, evidence that could be read as the residue of cooking fires or, indeed, fires burned for other purposes. At the end of his March digging, Harrington deduced that he had been dealing with "one main firepit in which building products from a 'settler's house' were used to support the pot."[127]

It later became clear that the pit was almost certainly of English origin and that it was located within a timber-cornered structure measuring approximately nine feet square. Two more pits were found within it, both with fragments of brick and burned clay in them. But it was the rectangular deposit that was, as Harrington described it, "the most interesting and important." The brick concentration also included a roofing tile fragment and a large ceramic sherd, the latter the neck from a sixteenth-century Normandy French stoneware flask known as Martincamp, of a type in use in the late sixteenth century. "This agglomeration," wrote Harrington, lay in a jumbled mass, as though it had been dumped in at random to form a base for some special feature, such as a forge. However, "the great quantity of Indian pottery mixed in with clay and scattered throughout the sunken square, is strong evidence that Indians were responsible for all three of the firepits."[128] It would seem, therefore, that Harrington had been drawn to a colonist attribution and then backed away from it on the evidence of an unspecified number of Indian sherds. He thought differently of the square structure, however.

The building, if such it was, defined itself by soil stains at its corners that Harrington identified as taproot holes, one of which was traced to a depth of five feet. "A similar condition was noted at another tree root area," he added, "and would seem to be a natural process of root decay and sand infiltration, although it looked very man-made." Harrington's puzzlement was understandable, for it seemed very unlikely that trees would be standing at exactly the right places to provide the builder with each of his four corners. Between the corner trees, Harrington found horizontal stains, which he identified as "almost certainly the molds of logs laid horizontally." More such logs were found extending winglike away from the square structure, interrupted at obtuse angles by more tree

The Martincamp stoneware flask found by Harrington in 1965. Partially restored. Height approx. 11 inches (27.94 cm.). *Public domain.*

rootholes. Outside this complex immediately to the north and appearing to wrap around it was a shallow ditch that yielded more sherds of the Normandy flask.[129]

In his report on these 1965 discoveries, Harrington put forward several explanations that ranged from an Indian sweat lodge to a small, timber-reinforced earthwork. "Another suggestion," he wrote, "has been made that the feature was associated with the [1587–88] palisaded village and that its closeness to the fort is simply a coincidence." He ended by concluding that for want of any more plausible interpretation, the structure "was contemporary with the fort and had some functional relation to it."[130]

The discovery of bricks within the "outwork" was rightly seen by Harrington as a discovery of major importance, made more so by the fact that some of the bats were broken from bricks that had been deliberately abraded to the point of being markedly concave on one side. Although appearing (in Harrington's opinion) to have been found in an Indian-created context (firepit), he concluded that the abrasion was the product of use "by the colonists for smoothing, polishing or sharpening purposes." He had earlier elaborated by noting that "armor needed polishing and weapons would require sharpening," and that "these relatively soft bricks would have been ideal for the purpose."[131]

Harrington later had the brick clay analyzed and determined that it was consistent with local sources, leaving little doubt that they were of Roanoke manufacture. This conclusion fitted historical evidence provided by the self-serving recollections of one David Glavin, an Irish soldier who told the Spaniards that he had been among Lane's 1585 settlers, who "as soon as they had disembarked…began to make brick and tiles for a fort and houses." Glavin's deposition went on to state that "he remained with them a year and a half until Francis Drake…arrived with his fleet."[132] In testimony recorded fourteen years later, Glavin's memory was evidently less sharp than it would have been earlier. His stay on Roanoke Island had been half the time he claimed. Thus his recollections about brick- and tile-making may have been equally faulty, for although the outwork's bricks were of local make, the tiles were not.

Archaeological confirmation that bricks were made by Raleigh's colonists was welcome and unequivocal, but the identification of the square structure and its log-laid wings was not as universally saluted. Located within about fifty feet of the rebuilt fort's rampart and less than forty from the ditch's outer edge, the outwork would seem to have been more an impediment to the defenders' field of fire than a useful advance position.[133] Had this structure been placed directly in front of the fort's entrance, the theory that it was an

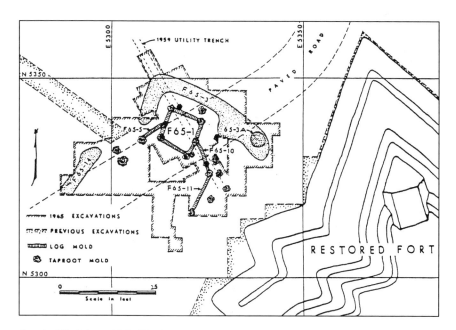

Opposite: Virginia and J.C. Harrington investigating the brick concentration first discovered in 1959. *NPS*.

Above: Harrington's outwork beside the restored earthwork. *Public domain*.

outwork would have made much better sense, but it was located well to the north of the rampart's opening.

Debate continued off and on through the next several years but always in the context of one anchoring certainty, namely, that the reconstructed earthwork was indeed Ralph Lane's fort—until 1978, when the park's unofficial historian, Phillip Evans, presented what seemed to be new evidence.

In 1976, the Colonial Williamsburg Foundation began excavations at Carter's Grove Plantation in James City County and there uncovered the remains of homes and communities associated with the circa 1619–45 settlement of Martin's Hundred. Among the most important discoveries was the layout of a wooden fort of post, rail and pale construction that possessed boxlike projecting flankers at two and possibly three of its corners. The fort had been erected in 1620, attacked by the Indians in 1622 and later used as a cattle compound. It protected the rear of Martin's Hundred's administrative center, Wolstenholme Towne, and served as a retreat for settlers living either in undefended homes or within secondary, probably breast-high, palisades. In short, Wolstenholme Towne was laid out on the standard Irish bawn village plan, a colonist settlement with an attached fortified residence for a senior officer and town militia force—also aping, perhaps, Ralph Lane's fort and settlement.

It was not this potential parallelism that attracted Phillip Evans's attention, however, but the fact that the plan of the Wolstenholme fort's largest flanker (interpreted by field archaeologist Eric Klingelhofer as a watchtower) matched Harrington's outwork post for post and foot for foot. Furthermore, the postern gate and lines of the Virginia fort's curtain walls bore a close resemblance to the Fort Raleigh outwork structure. Evans had no immediate explanation, but he had asked a highly relevant question: why?

Excited by Evans's discovery, the Fort Raleigh administrators, in February 1982, called a conference of individuals having some knowledge of the site's history and archaeology. It was a gathering led by historian David Quinn and archaeologist J.C. Harrington. For two days, the experts debated, putting forward first one theory and then another, not the least of them being Professor Quinn's suggestion that if Harrington's outwork was really

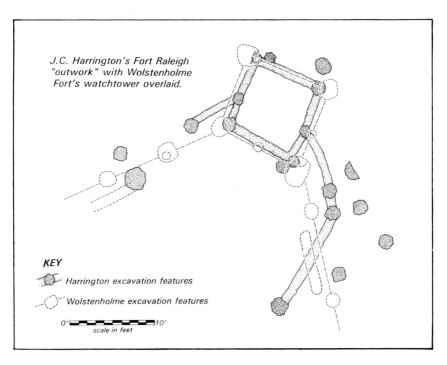

J.C. Harrington's Fort Raleigh
"outwork" with Wolstenholme
Fort's watchtower overlaid.

KEY

Harrington excavation features

Wolstenholme excavation features

0'   10'
scale in feet

Harrington's structural remains (stippled) overlaid with seemingly comparable posthole patterns of the circa 1620 palisaded fort at Wolstenholme Towne in Virginia. *Drawing by JM.*

the corner of a wooden fort (possibly Lane's weak wooden structure), then the earthwork might be one of three or more connected by curtain palisades to create the defense work seen by White in 1590. Although it seemed highly unlikely that such a flanker would take the closed form of the reconstructed earthwork, the fact that insufficient digging had been done around it to prove that no palisades stretched away from it prevented the theory from being discarded along with the others. The assembled pundits readily supported the Park Service's proposal to undertake a remote sensing survey of the area around and beyond the reconstructed fort, with particular emphasis on the environs of Harrington's outwork.

This work was led by Park Service archaeologists John E. Ehrenhard and William P. Athens and included not only a proton magnetometer survey but also a soil resistivity study and photographic coverage that included infrared as well as regular black-and-white and color. In short, several search procedures unavailable to Harrington in the 1947–50 investigations were brought to bear on the Fort Raleigh site. Initial results were encouraging, and one interpretation of the plotted anomalies suggested the presence of "up to six structures occurring in two parallel lines with a 'road' leading to them from the fort entrance."[134] Unfortunately, initial testing by excavation failed to confirm this tentative finding.

The test digging conducted by Ehrenhard and his colleagues, although of the highest standard, was unable to make much of anything. Several of the tree hole/burned post features of the kind previously encountered by Harrington and earlier by Talcott Williams were found and sectioned. Charcoal from three possible postholes was carbon-14 tested only to yield singularly unhelpful results that put all three several centuries before the English occupation.[135] Convinced that something was wrong, Ehrenhard had samples tested for contaminants at the School of Forestry at the University of Florida, but without learning anything conclusive. It fell to the ever-probing Phillip Evans to discover that in an effort to kill insects and weeds, the park's acres had been regularly sprayed with diesel fuel and malathion that could very well have contaminated the charcoal samples.

In the same year, Evans made two more significant discoveries. While walking the shore below the fort-supporting bluff during a low spring tide, he came upon the remains of two wood-lined wells about fifty feet from the cliff.[136] One was lined with an osier-hooped, stave-built barrel and the other with a hollowed log. Samples of these, too, were submitted for carbon-14 dating, and both yielded dates that could put them in the right period: the barrel AD 1285–1660 and the log AD 1340–1650. Ehrenhard noted that, though the dating emphasis was earlier than the 1580s, there seemed every chance that these discoveries were "associated with the 1587 colony and may be representative of wells located near the docking area."[137] The writer did not elaborate, but it seems fair to deduce that he was mindful of the Spaniard Vicente Gonzales's 1588 examination of a slipway and wells made from English casks, and it was for this reason that he connected Evans's wells with the 1587 settlement and not with Lane's, whose people could have dug wells reopened by White's.

The Park Service's 1982 survey was commendably thorough and included gathering soil samples that could be tested for organic phosphates, traces likely to be left by the body waste from the people living or working in the sampled areas. Again, the results were discouraging; Ehrenhard concluded that "either the sandy soils do not permit phosphates to fix and they leach out or that cultural activity in the area was minimal and cannot be identified."[138] Also tested were samples of the many ferric-appearing concretions of kinds previously noted by Harrington and, it is believed, by Williams. Radiographic prints failed to identify any forged iron fragments or, indeed, anything at all.[139]

Although the sum of the 1982 survey was less encouraging than the Park Service had hoped, funding was provided to enable the Ehrenhard team to return in 1983 to expand the previously limited areas of excavation as well as to undertake additional aerial photography. This time, the principal area of excavation would pursue previously plotted magnetic anomalies around Harrington's outwork. Although more tree holes/postholes were found and plotted and careful sectional drawings made, the holes created no clearly identifiable structural pattern. The sections (profiles) showed that the basic stratigraphy was the same as that recorded by Williams and Harrington. Summarizing the results of the 1983 digging, Ehrenhard wrote this: "The scarcity of colonial artifacts noted by Harrington seems to have been reaffirmed; a surface area of some 1120 square feet was opened during the 1983 season with only 3.2% of that area yielding any colonial artifacts."[140]

The artifact count and distribution may have appeared disappointing, but in truth, the range of fragments would prove to be the catalyst to carry the search for Ralph Lane's settlement into a new phase and down an unexpected path. Most of the potsherds came from a small test excavation ten feet south of the area opened by Harrington in 1965.[141] The thirty-eight fragments were divided into the following categories:

1. Salt-glazed stoneware	28.95%
2. Unglazed fine stoneware	5.26%
3. Coarse earthenware	13.16%
4. Green lead-glazed earthenware	5.26%
5. Tin enameled earthenware (majolica)	44.73%
6. Refined earthenware (pearlware)	2.63%

The last of these, the pearlware, came from an upper layer and could be discounted—at least as a dating determinant for the sherds from the other five categories.[142] Because none of the sherds were illustrated in the Ehrenhard report, the only means of learning more about them—short of having them returned from storage in Florida—was to try to draw conclusions from the written descriptions.

The first category, the "salt-glazed stoneware," included the statement: "Three of the fragments join together to form part of the rim section of a crucible-like vessel," prompting the question "Might it not be an actual crucible?"—in which case, the fragments are unlikely to be of salt-glazed stoneware. The second group, the "fine stoneware," was thought to "be similar to a type of stoneware known as basaltware." Taken at face value, therefore, these pieces should be associated with the pearlware, for basalt was a late-eighteenth-century refinement of a black-bodied, reduction-fired stoneware originally developed in England by David and John Biers at the end of the seventeenth century. Next, the lead-glazed earthenware, was first thought to be Spanish and then, perhaps, akin to something that had been found at Jamestown and Martin's Hundred, albeit as much as thirty-five years later.

The largest class, the "tin-enameled earthenware," was determined to "consist of a variety of Spanish majolica," prompting Ehrenhard to observe, "Having Spanish majolica as part of the historic ceramics collected at this English colonial site is both of interest and concern." Relying on Spanish ceramic expert Dr. Charles H. Fairbanks, who had written that majolica was largely a "luxury" item, Ehrenhard was prompted to speculate that the sherds came from "highly prize[d] possessions of one of the wealthier Roanoke colonists."[143] He also speculated that the majolica sherds, as well as the Iberian jar fragments found by Harrington, might have been "deposited by Spanish travelers on a visitation to the site after the abandonment of the Roanoke colony."[144] Ehrenhard came appreciably closer to the mark when he recalled that majolica sherds found by Harrington were thought to have come from a pharmaceutical jar and might be similar to the newly found

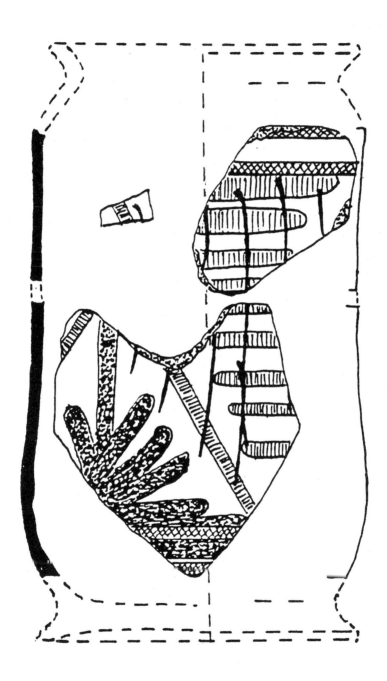

An Anglo-Netherlandish tin-glazed apothecary jar reconstructed from fragments found close to the Fort Raleigh earthwork. Original height 8". *Drawing by INH.*

pieces. Furthermore, Harrington's discovery of an apothecary's weight in the ditch fill might suggest that these artifacts, as well as the crucible-like rim, all shared a common purpose.

Of 198 fragments of aboriginal pottery recovered in the 1983 excavations, 141 came from the test excavation south of Harrington's 1965 area, and these were categorized as follows:

Colington Simple Stamped	*46*
Colington Plain	*35*
Colington Incised	*8*
Colington residual fragments	*52*[145]

With so large a number of Indian sherds found in association with the European material, Ehrenhard deduced that the Roanoke colonists were using aboriginal vessels to replace their own damaged ceramics. As alternatives, he suggested that this might be evidence that Indians were living in close association with the colonists or of their return to occupy the site after the colonists' departure.

Although the 1982–83 fieldwork at Fort Raleigh failed to provide a better understanding of Harrington's outwork or to close in on the site of Lane and White's settlement, it did contribute valuable data about the distribution of artifacts and hinted (correctly, as it would later turn out) at their origin and purpose. However, as is inevitable in archaeology, some assumptions would be proved wrong in the light of later knowledge—as would the possibility of there being a twin to the reconstructed earthwork in the middle of the Park Service's parking lot!

This revolutionary notion stemmed from the digital analysis of aerial photographs that showed a somewhat fort-like anomaly (complete with projecting flankers and entrance opening) that gave credence to David Quinn's suggestion that the reconstructed earthwork might have been but a corner of the palisaded enclosure seen by White in 1590.[146] Later testing of the anomaly failed to locate it and, subsequently, to dismiss it as a modern disturbance. That it was pursued at all is a measure of the open-minded approach of the Park Service in its desire to do whatever it could to unravel the riddle of Fort Raleigh.

Chapter 4

MORE ARCHAEOLOGY, 1991–93

In the half decade that followed the Ehrenhard excavations, much attention was being paid in Virginia to the interpretation of past and current archaeological excavations on early seventeenth-century sites. The writer was involved both in a reassessment of the reconstructed fort at Jamestown and with the analysis of the 1976–83 excavations at Wolstenholme Towne and elsewhere in Martin's Hundred. To better understand the kinds of palisades, breastworks, berms, sconces and the like constructed against both Indians and foreign invaders in Virginia, it seemed wise to return to the birthplace of British fort building in America—to Roanoke Island. To that end, then park superintendent Thomas Hartman was asked whether the Ehrenhard artifacts could be brought back from Florida and assembled alongside all Harrington's material in the hope of getting a better handle on the scope of the artifactual evidence.

Thanks to Mr. Hartman's cooperation as well as that of his assistant Bebe Woody, the artifacts were brought together, and in 1990, aided by the wise counsel of the late Audrey Noël Hume, the ceramic and other items were carefully reviewed. But care (though exercised) was not necessary to enable the messages to be read. Unless we were hopelessly adrift, the artifacts were speaking loudly and with clarity: virtually all could have been associated with the scientific researches of Thomas Harriot and metallurgist Joachim Gans. Ehrenhard had been right in identifying his joining sherds as pieces of crucibles but wrong in calling them salt-glazed stoneware, as they were refractory wares capable of withstanding high heat during alchemical processes. Dr. Fairbanks had been wrong in calling the tin-glazed earthenware Spanish majolica. The pieces, without recognizable exception, were of types and designs of Anglo-Netherlandish origin, and Ehrenhard had been correct in associating them with the crucible fragments, for all came from small pharmaceutical jars. The refined stoneware called basaltware by Ehrenhard turned out to be two fragments from a Martincamp flask like that found by Harrington in his outwork pit. The green-glazed earthenware fragments came from North Devon baluster jars, capable of use for general storage, that could have included laboratory materials.[147] Then, too, a reexamination of Harrington's outwork bricks strongly suggested that those that had been shaped to create one incuse side were not the chance product of sharpening swords or polishing armor but had been deliberately shaped to provide the round openings found on the tops and sides of metallurgical and distilling furnaces.[148]

As important as the artifacts found were those that were not. There were no redware cooking pots, no pans, no pitchers; nor were there any of the animal bones and shells normally associated with early European occupation. One might explain the absence of kitchenware by saying that colonists of the better sort ate from pewter and even silver cups, while the rest used treen (wooden vessels), none of which break into fragments likely to be found in the ground. The pewter and silver would be taken away, while wooden dishes, if left behind, would soon rot. But that is not true of food garbage. The bones and shells do survive in the earth, and no Indian would have carted them away.

So what did all this mean? First, nobody lived in the immediate vicinity of Harrington's outwork; second, the European ceramics were limited to crucibles, tin-glazed pharmaceutical pots, West of England jars and Martincamp flasks, all of which could have been used by Harriot and Gans. Couple the ceramic evidence with the shaped bricks and one has an associated forge or furnace and, by extension, a nearby workshop.[149] This all made good sense, save for one overriding objection. It seemed extremely unlikely that with all the island to build on, the scientific workshop would have been erected immediately outside the earthen fort. Harrington had in mind for his outwork some sort of dirt-embanked log- and tree-supported breastwork over which the fort's defenders could fire. But a workshop, roofed as it would have been, could have provided ideal cover for attacking Indians.

There was, however, another possibility based on another clue: namely, the lump of copper waste that Harrington had found under the rampart and so predated it. Rather than having been dropped there immediately upon Lane's arrival and before the "Newe Forte in Verginia" was up, perhaps the evidence was saying that the Harriot/Gans workshop area extended under and so predated the fort. This was an iconoclastic thesis, for if it could be proven, it would mean that the reconstructed earthwork could not be Ralph Lane's fort.

When this possibility was put to park superintendent Hartman, in spite of its disturbing implications, he was quick to agree that new excavations were needed to carry the investigation up to the edge of the reconstructed ditch to try to determine whether or not it cut through the spread of the Harriot/Gans workshop's debris.[150]

PHASE 1: THE PREVIEW

A prerequisite for any successful archaeology is that the director knows what he or she is doing, and that necessitates being acquainted with the ground and the demands that it will impose on personnel, on equipment and, most importantly, on the budget. To this end, the Virginia Company Foundation, with the writer as director, undertook in 1991 a test excavation adjacent to the area impacted by Harrington's 1965 excavation and another to relocate his backfilled area.[151] First, however, the park area immediately west of the earthwork was resurveyed, the trees located and, where possible, old datum points relocated. With that done, the Virginia Company crew set up grid lines and used those to control the placement of one three-foot-by-ten-foot test trench and the first of three ten-foot square-based area excavations.[152] (For excavation units and features, excluding the "charcoal pit," please refer to the site map located on pages 6–7.)

The site for the test trench (E.R.3) was chosen to be adjacent to the 1965 Harrington excavation but, at the same time, sufficiently distant not to have been disturbed by grading after he was through. Its purpose was to examine the stratigraphic sequence described by Williams and his successors. There—in a preview of much to come—the ground had been damagingly impacted by twentieth-century activities, notably by the destruction of an asphalt-based roadway (in 1964?) and by the laying of an earlier waterline into the reconstructed fort. Where the pre–Park Service stratigraphy survived, the sequence was clear enough: beginning an average of nine inches below the modern surface was a six-to-seven-inch layer of gray sandy loam (E.R.3D) that blended into a more-than-one-inch stratum of brown sand flecked with charcoal (E.R.3G), below which stretched a primary layer of brown sand (E.R.3J) about nine inches in thickness before blending into the natural sandy clay subsoil. Artifacts were woefully scarce and were limited to two small sherds of Colington series Indian pottery in the D layer overlying the charcoal-flecked stratum immediately west of the reconstructed earthwork.

The trench's principal feature was the massive waterline trench that occupied most of its southern end, but in the side of which was what appeared to be an ash-flecked post mold.[153] A slice through the top of the soil-filled hole survived in the side of the utility trench, and when carefully cleaned and the fill removed, it appeared to have the straight edge that usually distinguishes a man-made hole from a natural transformation around a growing tree. The mold continued below the bottom of the utility trench and disappeared at a depth of 4' 10" below modern grade. Because most structural holes rarely go beyond two or three feet in depth—and many less—this seemed incredibly deep and left the excavators wondering whether it was, after all, no more than the remains of a tree's taproot. At the same time, one remained mindful of William Strachey's 1610 description of the palisades at Jamestown, which were, he said, set "foure foote deepe in the ground."[154] Was this, we wondered, an example of the conveniently placed corner trees that had supported Harrington's outwork?

Concurrently with digging the test trench, an area excavation was opened to locate the southwest corner of Harrington's 1965 excavation (F.R.E.R.2).

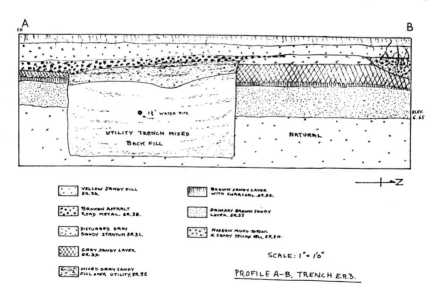

Field-drawn eight-foot-long profile along first 1991 test trench west of Harrington's 1965 features. The right-side stratigraphy is typical of the layering throughout the area. *FCF*

Harrington was renowned as a careful recorder, and his investigated area turned out to be exactly where he had plotted it—an assurance that boded well for the future (E.R.2). The removal of enough of his backfill to define the edges yielded a rim sherd from a tin-glazed ointment pot of the kind that Ehrenhard had found in unit M.S.10. This discovery was an important reminder that Harrington's excavation had been undertaken in a hurry-up mode that prevented him from screening all his dirt. It seemed highly likely, therefore, that other sherds—perhaps many other sherds—had been shoveled back. Consequently, the new excavations would have to include the careful removal of Harrington's backfill from his entire 1963 area of excavation. Although not the best of news, this meant that more important artifactual evidence might be recovered from the outwork area and that the Virginia Company team would then have the opportunity to reexamine Harrington's enigmatic outwork and its tree/postholes.

A second area excavation (E.R.6) designed to locate the northern edge of the Ehrenhard area opened in 1983 was equally successful, although the cut provided more evidence of the damage done to the site by its custodians. Another utility trench sliced across the area, carrying a board-covered electrical line to a series of walkway lights flanking the concrete paved path that approached the fort from the southwest. Nature, too, had done its damage, a tree's root system occupying much of the opened area. A third test unit (E.R.7) was opened against the edge of the concrete walkway, only to reveal that the crushed rock bed of an older pavement, as well as the root system for a large tree, had destroyed all but a few inches of the assumed sixteenth-century sequence.[155] Nevertheless, the early layers did continue beneath the paved walk—the same paved walk that fronted the reconstructed fort's ditch. To accomplish what needed to be done, the concrete paving would have to be removed. It said much for the level of Park Service cooperation that this request was received with undismayed acceptance. The pavement would be gone before the Virginia Company team returned on October 25, 1991.

PHASE 2: THE SEARCH EXPANDED

With the site fully gridded—at least on paper—and with the crew greatly enlarged, twenty-three squares were opened either in part or in their entirety during sixteen days of uninterrupted excavation. Fourteen passed with

The earthwork under reconstruction in 1950. *NPS.*

ever-increasing despondency, nine-tenths of the ground having either been disturbed by root action and a variety of modern intrusions or being barren save for the occasional small prehistoric sherd akin to those found in the first April test trench. All attempts to find the Elizabethan strata cut through by the fort ditch failed. As suspected (and as the 1950 photographs indicated), the ground beyond the ditch had been churned up to a disfiguring degree.

A trench surrounding a rectangular clay platform to the southwest of the studied area held early promise, particularly when the same sandy clay stratum below the trench yielded several flaking fragments of soft brick akin to those found by Harrington in his outwork pit.[156] The reason for the brick's presence was never resolved, but the central platform with its enclosing ditch was convincingly determined. Photographs shot in 1951 soon after the fort was reconstructed showed visitors reading the 1896 Virginia Dare monument, which had been moved from inside the fort to this location (see photograph on page 79.)[157]

In an attempt to reexamine Harrington's outwork, a partial overlying grid square was opened and found to contain much modern asphalt and

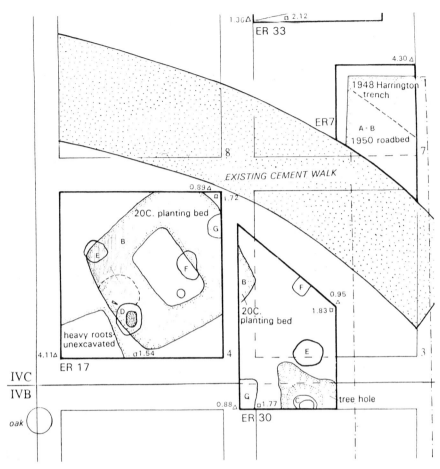

Detail of the 1991 excavation plan showing the Virginia Dare monument girdling trench and at "D" the area of colonial brick debris below it. Units are eight-foot squares in ten-foot blocks. *Plan by JM.*

assorted debris, presumably trucked in at the close of the 1965 excavation.[158] Although Harrington and his wife, Virginia, visited the site on November 6 and 7, neither could throw any light on what was left of their outwork traces.[159] A randomly selected test unit to relocate a Harrington trench dating from 1947 toward the northwest corner of the gridded area yielded a single fragment from a large crucible, suggesting that Gans-related artifacts were more widely scattered than had hitherto been expected.[160]

Although a prodigious number of squares were opened, and many natural (tree-related) features were laboriously excavated and their merits debated at unjustifiable length, the only such features unequivocally

Part of the 1991 excavation area with square F.R.E.R. 8 in the foreground. At right is the edge of the remaining strip of the Science Center floor, to its left post holes along the Park Service road (see figure on page 102), and in front the south edge of J.C. Harrington's 1965 excavation. View from the North. *NPS.*

recognizable were the once-replaced postholes for a low guardrail that defined the ditch-side edge of a circa-1950 road that crossed square III.C.9 from west to east. Photographs taken before and after the reconstruction showed first unconnected waist-high posts and then shorter posts with a capping rail, an evolution that no archaeologist who sees only round holes in the ground could ever accurately reconstruct (see photograph above). This was a sobering demonstration of archaeology's limitations and of the fact that one photograph shot in the right place at the right time can be worth a thousand dug holes.

The same square that exposed the roadside ditch was also to yield a significant number of Elizabethan-period artifacts, although several of them came from the silting of that ditch—in association with modern bottle glass and a .22 shell casing. Among the early fragments were Martincamp flask sherds, more crucible pieces and one sherd from a North Devon baluster jar.[161] A thin lens of black sand immediately under the modern ditch yielded Indian sherds and a fragment of brick.[162] This stratum of black sandy loam

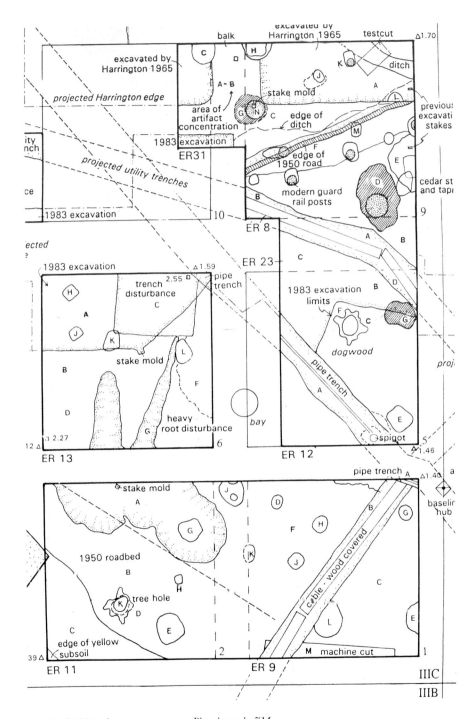

Detail of 1991 science center area. *Plan drawn by JM.*

extended to and settled into a deep taproot hole that yielded only charcoal but whose overlying layer of sandy loam contained an iron fishhook,[163] the only tin-glazed sherd found in the phase 2 digging and what appeared to be a small lump of cuprous waste.[164] At the east edge of the square adjacent to the taproot lay a deposit of mottled brown sandy loam that yielded two fragments of an Indian tobacco pipe.[165]

Square III.D.9 had been disturbed not only by the laying, fencing and removal of the modern road but also by the southern extremity of Harrington's 1965 excavation. Part of the square's southern upper levels had been previously excavated during the 1983 Ehrenhard investigation, and two of his five-meter survey stakes were encountered cutting into Harrington's backfill and into the artifact-bearing deposit (E.R.8E).

The area of significance (i.e., the sandy layers yielding sixteenth-century artifacts) extended south from square III.D.9, beyond the east-west balk into square III.C.5, which, although sliced by the waterline trench first encountered in the April test cut, revealed a layer of gray sandy loam from which came several small Indian sherds, a small iron object of uncertain character and, most importantly, a mini-bar of worked antimony, a mineral used in metallurgical assays.[166]

This square and its northerly balk were both exposing the same, occasionally ash-flecked, layer that was simultaneously being uncovered beneath and adjacent to the roadside ditch.[167] Some unnecessary hesitancy attended this area of excavation because the Ehrenhard excavation of 1983 should, so we thought, have removed this stratum, and yet its uniformity suggested otherwise. It turned out that the 1983 excavations had not been carried to undisturbed subsoil and, in a crucial area yet to be found, had stopped two inches above it.

Elsewhere, the backfilled spoil of past excavations, coupled with a miscellany of other modern disturbances, continued to bedevil the Virginia Company archaeologists, causing morale to continue to decline. The National Geographic Society's assigned photographer added to the gloom by constantly complaining that there was nothing for him to photograph. He would leave early on the Friday of the dig's last scheduled day, as would the Park Service's archaeological representative Bennie Keel—several hours before the discovery was made that rendered all the fruitless labor eminently worthwhile.

The story of twentieth-century discovery at Fort Raleigh had always been low-key—no chests of colonists' abandoned armor, no skeletons pierced by arrows, no stolen silver cups or even a discarded quarterdeck gun. As Talcott Williams had observed, "the site proved singularly barren of debris."[168] That complaint was echoed by Harrington and later by Ehrenhard, who stated that "the scarcity of colonial artifacts noted by Harrington seems to have been confirmed."[169] But had Ehrenhard continued a little longer and a little deeper, his artifact tally would have appreciably increased. The directorial daybook entry, written while the importance of the discovery was still unfolding, described it thus:

> *Promise of rain and another Nor'easter hastened the excavation to near completion by the end of the day. This proved to be the most rewarding of the expedition when Wm. Kelso's baulk excavation III C. 9/10 yielded approximately forty artifacts scattered on an original C.16 land surface which had miraculously escaped both Harrington's and Ehrenhard's excavations. The finds included the first glass fragments to be found at the site and the earliest English glass (?) discovered in the New World.[170] Among other finds were chips of white flint, sherds of crucible and costrel [Martincamp flask], as well as pieces of charcoal and Indian potsherds. This scatter unquestionably represents part of the workplace of Joachim Gans and confirms his activity within the "Outwork."…At the day's end the feared rain had not started, but the wind was rising and very cold.*

Work had ended in all the opened areas save for the Gans workshop sector, the bottoms of the squares being lined with black plastic prior to mechanical backfilling. A 1991 penny was placed in each area below the plastic to enable future excavators to determine not only where the digging had halted (usually at the natural subsoil) but also when. The daybook entry for Saturday, November 9, continued like this:

> *Daylight revealed that the weather had deteriorated and was getting worse. But the site had suffered little damage. Only Audrey Noël Hume's work tent had blown down.…Dr. Kelso's area IIIC 9/10 which had been rich in artifacts yesterday afternoon proved more so today. Among the finds was the largest fragment of crucible yet recovered from any of the excavations, a sizeable piece of glass with recognizable curvature, a large fragment of the costrel, also an Indian pipe-stem fragment, a small brass ring, several pieces of English flint, and two nuts, also a piece of partially carbonized pine wood.[171] There was no doubt that this narrow balk left behind by Harrington had given us part of Gans's and Harriot's workshop floor. The digging finally ended (as the rain came down harder and the wind grew more vigorous) at about 1:40 p.m.*

Not mentioned in that summary were several small scales of iron rust. Many more had been found in the abutting area to the south (12C). At first, they seemed to be of no significance, but as more and more were found, they began to establish an artifactual entity of their own—as did the distribution of white flint chips. Later documentary research would show that the iron scales were not random flakes of rust from the cleaning of, say, a corroding cannon but were, instead, part of an assayer's or other furnace user's equipment. Randle Home's *Academy of Armory* (1682) described how distilling components were joined together using a mortar called "the Lute of wisdom" and made from a mixture of "pouder of Tyles or well burnt bricks, the pouder of Iron scales and fine sand…and other ingredients each a like quantity."[172]

The orderly progression of the 1991 excavations required that the limits of each removed segment be controlled by the pattern of the grid. Thus Dr. Kelso's square III.C.9 had been carried westward to take in a six-foot north/south segment of balk 9/10 and two feet of the adjacent square no. 10. That extension revealed that the undisturbed ground was largely limited to a three-foot balk left by Harrington in 1965 that had provided him with his survey line but beyond which the ground had been disturbed to the natural subsoil and then backfilled.[173] To the north, however, Harrington's balk—and, in it, the undisturbed workshop floor—extended into the face of the excavation and beneath the roots of a small tree. Because his plan showed

The 1991 Science Center excavations in the background, with the west rampart of the earthwork in the foreground. *FCF.*

the entire area to have been excavated, there was no knowing how much further the "good ground" continued. But on a closing Saturday afternoon and with the crew disbanded, there could be no finding out. Whatever additional information lay to the north would remain there for another year, another dig—and another fundraising effort.

Raising money for archaeology is never easy, and at Fort Raleigh, the Park Service's tight budget and the heavy, often weather-driven demands of a national park that encompassed much more than the fort site meant that its support, of necessity, was limited to labor and equipment. To potential donors, however, the fact that the U.S. Department of the Interior was not supporting the project monetarily had, from the outset, been a high hurdle to o'erleap. That the end of the 1991 season had so discouraged the National Geographic Society's photographer that he packed up and left before the end boded ill for any further help from that all-important source. There seemed but one way to compensate for the fact that the largest discovered treasure was a crucible sherd barely two inches long: if the end product did not look important, it had to *sound* important. Going out on an attenuated limb, this director declared to the local press (and later in a National Geographic Society news release) that the 1991 excavations had discovered "America's First Science Center"—the place where the story of England in the New World really began.

Claiming to be, or to have, the first of anything can get one into trouble, and in this case, it did. Dr. William Fitzhugh, director of the Smithsonian Institution's Baffin Island studies of Martin Frobisher's Arctic expeditions of 1576–78, was quick to point out that those voyagers had included a scientific component. Like Raleigh's Germanic Joachim Gans, Frobisher's metallurgical team had been headed by another German, one Jonas Schutz.[174] Valid though that response was, the Fort Raleigh workplace suggested usage broader than Gans's metallurgy. Knowing that Harriot had assembled botanical specimens and that he was experienced in the use of furnaces and distilling apparatus, the nuts and seeds found on the floor were seen as evidence of the area's multidisciplinary use—hence the Science Center appellation.

Colleagues spared the task of funding another season's excavation were more cautious and may have felt that grandiose claims should wait until the end. Nevertheless, the Science Center bait generated national publicity and led to a second National Geographic Society grant and to the renewal of sufficient others to get the team back in the field in 1992.

Although the 1991 season had failed to prove whether the Science Center activity area had been cut through by the diggers of the fort ditch,

Right: The remains of the 1936 Fort Raleigh palisade exposed in unit II.B.12. Beyond, to the east, lies the entrance to the earthwork rebuilt in 1950. *FCF.*

Below: A rotting post (1) provides food for tree roots (2), which grow larger as the post is consumed and the posthole edges are obscured (3–4), until the root system dies to be replaced by another, destroying any last trace of the original post and hole (5). *Sketch by INH.*

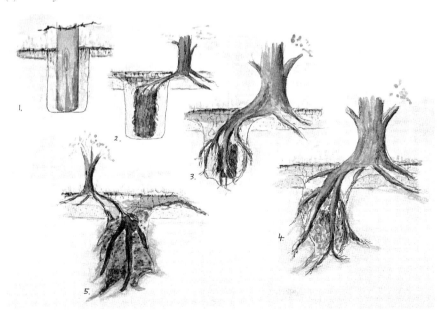

the attempt to do so yielded an unexpected bonus. Immediately west of the earthwork's entrance, a test cut revealed a section of the sawn-off 1936 palisade, one of whose juniper posts had been embraced by the nutrient-milking roots of a nearby, and still growing, live oak. Here was a classic and hitherto unrecorded example of the way in which decaying wood- and loam-filled post molds attract living plants whose root systems eventually distort and even obliterate the angular patterns of spade-dug postholes.

At the Fort Raleigh site, where the topsoil is thin and the subsoil fast draining, trees and lesser plants seek out every available source of nourishment, in time turning man-dug postholes into tree root systems. Here, therefore, was proof that Harrington had been right when he identified the remains of his outwork's supports as tree roots. Time and nature had played a trick that had baffled Harrington in 1965 and one that would continue to bedevil every subsequent Fort Raleigh archaeologist now and in the future.

Reassuring though the post-eating tree discovery had been—insofar that it explained how the outwork had been constructed—its message and broader implications were disturbing. The 1991 excavations had located and plotted in excess of one hundred holes, few if any of them with the neatly squared outer definition and the circular inner of the standard posthole/post mold relationship. Some holes, like those of the roadside guard rails, were recognizably modern and could be eliminated from the dot-connecting puzzle, but many more could not.[175] Because growing roots make no distinction between inhabiting colonial or prehistoric post placements and taking over the rotted root systems of older trees, the archaeologist has no way of knowing which holes had started as Raleigh-period features and which had not. Because it is a hoary axiom that any two dots (or post stains) can make a straight line, the site's possible permutations were endless. In contrast, Harrington's archaeological maps showed that two of his trenches west and southwest from the fort had revealed well-defined posthole/post mold units far more structural in appearance than anything found in 1991, and these features cried out to be reexamined in 1992.[176]

Phase 3: The 1992–93 Seasons

Two goals formed the basis for the second season's planning: pursuing Harrington's artifact-rich balk to its end and opening squares inside the fort in search of evidence that the Gans/Harriot work area extended beyond the earthwork's ditch or, alternatively, to find traces of in-fort occupation that had escaped Harrington's attention. That this last might be a possibility in no way questioned his objectivity. It stemmed from the fact that his plan of the fort showed three areas that had been unavailable for investigation due to the presence of root systems from trees cut down in 1950 (see figure on page 65).

The crew was the same that had accomplished so much in the previous season and brought back two of the 1991 servitors, whose gained experience now enabled them to be assisting excavators.[177] Still unable to contribute in currency, park superintendent Hartman agreed to provide servitor-level labor, and the Southeast Regional Center sent back the ever-valuable Bennie Keel and with him three Florida-based assistants who had yet to gain experience on a site as friable and disturbed as the Science Center sector of Fort Raleigh. Because the underlying premise for the entire excavation had been that the digging would be done only by people with related site experience, it was decided that Keel—being a Park Service archaeologist and the fort a Park Service reconstruction— and his crew should take responsibility for work within the earthwork, while the Virginia Company team would continue to focus on and around Harrington's outwork.

The season began with the simultaneous opening of three ten-foot squares in the center of the fort and with the removal of 1991 backfill from the key Science Center area south of Harrington's outwork.[178] At the same time, the maple whose roots partially covered the northerly balk was cut down to enable hand digging around its stump. Digging under it was a slow and time-consuming exercise but necessary to prevent the stump's removal from tearing up the Gans ground beneath it. The caution, though unavoidable, proved almost unnecessary.

Harrington's artifact-rich layer extended only eighteen inches into the balk before being sliced through by his outwork excavation. But care was not entirely wasted, for the careful digging and screening of Harrington's backfill provided a dramatic reminder of the fact that, when excavating his outwork, he had been under too much pressure to take the time to screen his dirt. The 1992 daybook entry for October 27 contained the following:

> *A surprising number of Elizabethan artifacts were recovered from the backfill. A pre-washing count suggests 17 aboriginal sherds, 20 crucible fragments, 5 pieces of flint, and 1 West of England sherd, one micaceous palette fragment and 42 costrel sherds. Also one piece of English roofing tile.*

Although more artifacts reflecting the same range of material were found in clearance immediately west and south of the outwork excavation, the presence of overlapping utility line trenches, along with the disturbances caused by the Ehrenhard excavations, ensured that few sherds were unequivocally lying in an undisturbed sixteenth-century stratum. In reality, however, the fact that so many of the ceramic fragments were out of context was relatively unimportant, there having been no English sixteenth- or seventeenth-century occupation after the departure of White's colonists. The sherds were all recognizably "of the period" and so could be assessed as such. What was lost, however, and tragically so, was the presence of datable artifacts in contexts that might have had something to say about the many root hole/posthole structural features—if, indeed, they were structural.

Square III.C.10, which was located immediately west of Harrington's preserved balk, had evidently been rich in evidence. But, as noted above, the damage done by utility-line installations, the Park Service's road ditch and its two archaeological excavations (1965 and 1983) left little in situ but the southwest corner that yielded a shallow depression heavy with charcoal and containing several aboriginal sherds. To the east of it, a small area of a stratum akin to that of the workshop floor had been cut through by a clearer-than-average posthole/post mold, in the east side of which were imbedded a lump of copper waste and a neck fragment from a wide-mouthed glass pharmaceutical flask. This last was found to join to another fragment found on the workshop floor at the end of the 1991 season.[179] Here, as perhaps nowhere else, one felt the anger of frustration at not being the first to uncover and interpret the workshop remains.

Although nothing was found that could identify the size or shape of buildings (or even that there were buildings other than Harrington's nine-foot Wolstenholme-like structure), square III.C.10 did provide a clue to their demise. A sloping-sided feature with a faint central discoloration suggestive of a two-phase unit is believed to have been a posthole.[180] Flecks and fragments of charcoal sloped downward from the sides, suggesting that they had been borne down when a post was pushed back and forth in the sandy fill to enable it to be pulled out. This could relate to John White's 1590 statement that he found the houses razed down and to the theory that structural timbers were salvaged by those of his settlers who went south to the Croatoans to await the arrival of the 1588 fleet that never came.

The complete removal of Harrington's backfill from the area west of his outwork revealed that his excavation had been taken deep into the subsoil over much of the area and cut through the remains of his outwork-girdling

Flask glass and worked copper in situ in an undisturbed fragment of the Science Center floor. F.R.E.R. 31B. View from the North. *FCE*

ditch extension.[181] Although Harrington had reported finding fragments of Martincamp flask in ditch fill closer to the nine-foot structure, no more pieces were found. However, two fragments of English roofing tile were recovered. Neither exhibited any attached mortar or evidence of burning, and so there was no knowing how, or if, the tiles had been used.

Similar tile fragments have been found at the Frobisher site on Kodlunarn Island. Writing about these, Reginald Auger of the Universitée Laval at Quebec said this:

> *Earthenware tiles are part of the hardware used in assay furnaces. They are used in clay furnaces for the same purpose as a bed-plate is used in the iron assay furnace....Two tiles are used so that when the upper one is damaged by the heat of the fire (a frequent event) it can easily be replaced with the other one.*

But having said this and more, Auger allowed that the red tiles' "abundance suggests that [they] could have been roofing tiles to cover some of the shelters built on the island."[182] Either or both interpretations could apply to the Fort Raleigh tiles—with equally inconclusive justification.

With the exception of its northern extremity, the western section of Harrington's ditch had been dug out by deep excavating in 1965. Additional

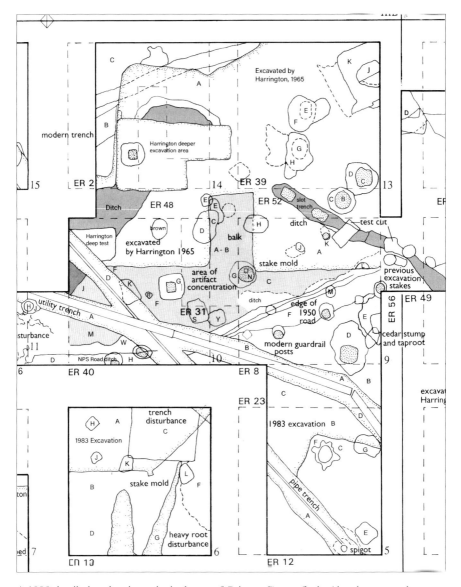

A 1992 detail plan showing principal area of Science Center finds. Also shown are the previously unexcavated sections of Harrington's westerly ditch (in dark gray) and the possibly related slot to its right. *Plan by JM.*

traces were found extending a further two feet in a southwesterly direction beyond the edge of his excavation. But although another area was opened to the west in the hope of finding more, massive modern road and tree root disturbances had eradicated all traces.[183] Perhaps coincidentally—and perhaps not—the previously mentioned brick fragments found beneath the 1896 monument platform lay on much the same southwest/northeast line as the tile-bearing ditch, suggesting (but by no means proving) that the ditch had enclosed the area of the Harriot/Gans scientific operation.

While there is no doubt that the ditch was contemporary with the outwork, its purpose remains obscure. Harrington was correct in recording a definite break in the line west of his structure, and one is tempted to see that as an entrance into some once-defined area. Three feet to the east and at a right angle to the head of the ditch extension ran a narrow and deep slot that was traced for a distance of seven feet before being lost into a tree-capped and thus unexcavated area.[184] Patches of loam in the sandy clay of the slot's fill suggested that grasses had grown in it, promoting the possibility that it had been a dripline cutting outside a building. Unfortunately, most of this intriguing slot lay beneath the bottom of Harrington's 1965 excavation, meaning that any other associated features had already been removed.

There can be no doubt that the principal area of scientific study was concentrated south of Harrington's outwork structure. Work-related debris was to be found in disturbed ground in testing further to the north as well as to the south, but always in insignificant quantities and in unstratified contexts.[185] Nevertheless, there was clear evidence that another, albeit quasi-scientific, activity had taken place approximately 145 feet to the south-southwest of the outwork. In a trench dug in 1947, Harrington had come upon a deep pit containing concentrated charcoal, which he described as follows:

> *The bottom 2 feet of the pit was a solid mass of charcoal, made from unsplit pine sticks from 1 to 4 inches in diameter. Some showed ax marks on the chopped ends, and none of the original pieces appeared to have been much longer than 1 foot. There was evidence of heat on the sides and bottom of the pit, but no ashes were found. Quite clearly, this pit was dug and used for the express purpose of making charcoal, although this is not known to have been a common method, even in those days. No cultural material was found in the pit, so, short of possible future dating by the tree-ring method, its age cannot be determined.[186]*

Harrington was writing prior to 1962, before radiocarbon (carbon-14) dating was widely available.[187] To obtain samples, lead archaeologists Eric Klingelhofer and Nick Luccketti were given the unenviable task of re-excavating part of Harrington's 1947 trench. A large pile of

Above: J.C. Harrington's 1947 trench reopened to further study his "charcoal pit" (*foreground*) and to recover charcoal samples from the pile thrown up into the trench. View from the West. *FCF.*

Opposite: The process of charcoal burning as illustrated in Denis Diderot's *Dictionnaire Des Sciences*, under "Oeconomie Rustique, Charbon de Bois." Figure 3 shows the caking of stacked faggots with clay. *Public domain.*

displaced charcoal was found in the backfilling of the trench, and more was discovered in the bottom of the pit where Harrington had left it. Fragments of red-fired clay were found amid the displaced charcoal and one apparent fragment of brick, but no surviving traces of the burning of the pit walls that Harrington had noted. On the contrary, the available evidence suggested that the charcoal had been thrown into the hole cold and that the burned clay and brick came from the dismantling of a mud-coated charcoal burner's dome.

The usual and simplest method of making charcoal was to set a pole vertically in the ground and build up billets of wood around it in four or five stages, depending on the diameter of the base, until a slightly stepped cone was created. The exterior was next coated with turf or clay to seal the heat within, whereupon the pole was extracted, and the resulting hole filled with burning charcoal. The entire structure then burned from within, slowly collapsing on itself. When the pile was no longer smoking, the workers pulled it apart. Debris remaining after the bulk of the charcoal sticks had been salvaged would consist of broken pieces of wood and the scorched clay from the sealing coat—residue similar to that found in the deep pit.[188] As Harrington did not describe or document the belowground method of charcoal burning that he believed paralleled his interpretation, it is impossible to endorse or to dismiss it. But as Harrington himself allowed, the technique "was not known to have been a common method, even in those days."

Although many of the remaining charcoal pieces exhibited the chopping marks previously described by Harrington, more of the fragments came from relatively light wood and not from the uniformly cut three-foot billets generally used for the method described above. There was, however, another method that was favored for small kindling-type charcoal. The wood was simply burned in an open fire, with water being ladled onto it from nearby tubs. But here, again, there is no mention of burning the charcoal in a deep pit, and the discovery of the burned clay lumps seems to point to the former, more controlled method of making charcoal. That samples recovered from the pit were of the Fort Raleigh period there could be no doubt. Carbon-14 testing provided an almost ideal bracket of AD 1450–1660.

The large number of charcoal pieces found in the immediate Science Center area left no doubt that charcoal was used there. However, the tested pieces were all pine, as were those from the Harrington pit, and pine was not the wood of choice for either iron- or other metalworkers, oak, beech and alder being preferred.[189] It has generally been assumed that trials of iron were made at the Fort Raleigh site, and well they may have been. But Harriot did not specifically say so. "In two places of the country specially," he wrote, "one about fourscore and the other six score miles from the Fort or place where wee dwelt: wee founde neere the water side the ground to be rockie, which by the trial of a minerall man, was founde to holde Iron richly."[190] Nothing is said about the samples being brought back to the settlement for smelting, and it remains possible that, as Harriot himself stated, testing was done at the water's edge by "the vertue of the loadstone in drawing yron."[191] Nevertheless, the next logical step would be to try to smelt the samples to determine the quality of the extractable metal. Although no inventories have been found to tabulate the equipment carried to Virginia either in 1585 or in 1587, we do know that Frobisher's third arctic expedition (1578) was supplied with large quantities of the necessary hardware:

> *Iron bars and plates…to construct 3 iron furnaces for small assays.*
> *2 iron stoves.*
> *223 earthenware pots* [crucibles?] *for 8 stoves.*[192]

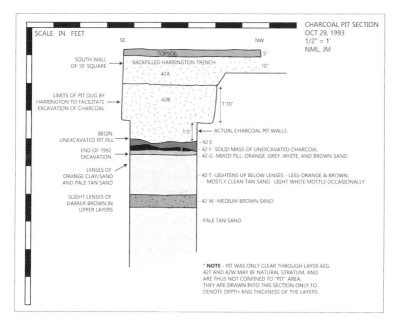

A section through Harrington's "charcoal pit" carried down into the natural substrata, by JM. *FCF*

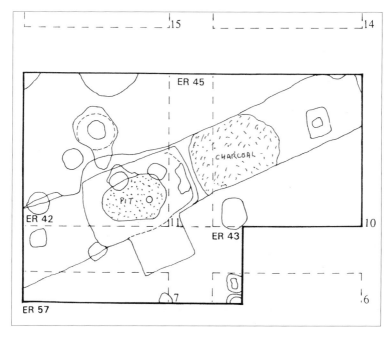

Field-drawn detail plan showing the charcoal-containing pit and to its right the pile of redeposited charcoal. *FCF*

Several postholes were found in the fifteen-foot-square excavation around Harrington's charcoal-rich pit, one of which yielded several large nodules that were thought to be bog iron and thus evidence of smelting in its immediate vicinity.[193] It was later determined, however, that the nodules contained no iron and were only much larger versions of the small concretions first encountered by Talcott Williams and by every excavator thereafter.

The pit was excavated in its entirety—and far below. Drainage through the charcoal had discolored the very sandy subsoil, raising the possibility that the feature was really the top of a backfilled well, a thesis encouraged by the mixed appearance of the strata, but it turned out to be geological rather than man created.[194]

In sum, all that could be said of the "charcoal pit" area was that charcoal had been burned nearby, probably by the usual covered-cone method, and that the procedure had been part of the Science Center activity. Whether the charcoal was used solely in the assaying furnaces or whether it also served an as-yet-undiscovered iron smelting venture remains to be determined by future archaeologists. As for the pit itself, its purpose, too, remains an enigma. Clearly, however, this southwesterly sector of the park deserves further careful investigation and should be protected from any more of the landscaping improvements that so severely damaged the outwork and its environs.

The 1992 season's simultaneous exploration within the fort led to the opening of four complete and two partial grid squares—with results that were both puzzling and eminently rewarding.[195] Although the backfilling of Harrington's excavations and grading for the reconstruction had done much to obscure the shapes and extent of features that had been better defined when he did his work, a key feature remained undisturbed: namely, the brick base for the 1896 Virginia Dare memorial. Harrington's plan published in 1962 showed a cluster of features in the center of the fort, under and abutting the cobblestone footing for the 1936 blockhouse—among them the memorial's footing.[196] Next in retrograde sequence were two large rectangular pits, which he identified only as recent deep intrusions (see map on page 65). One of these was partially re-excavated and found to contain modern bottle glass, barbed wire and, at the bottom, a well-preserved plank.[197]

Harrington had noted that the pit cut through one of Williams's 1895 excavations, thus bracketing it to 1895–1936, and in a later Note Book entry suggests that both large pits were "where some dogwood trees were taken out and moved when the blockhouse was built."[198] Nevertheless, the tested pit cut into a narrow feature that Harrington dubbed the "oldest

The 1992 earthwork interior excavations seen from the east. *FCF.*

Square I.B.15 excavated within the earthwork in 1992 exposing the original brick foundation for the 1896 monument. View from the East. *FCF.*

disturbance inside the fort" and that also had been cut into by two of Williams's 1895 tests.[199]

The early feature had been traced by Harrington for a distance of approximately 35'00" but seemingly lost its ends at north and south into tree-rooted areas that could not be excavated. The 1992 excavation faced no such limitation and enabled the feature to be pursued a little further—to 39'6"—and to ends that were truly its own. Due to backfilling and grading, the feature had lost the clean lines drawn by Harrington, but setting aside the variety of filling deposits (which often gave the appearance of antiquity until modern bottle glass and nails turned up in them), it is reasonable to conclude that Harrington's oldest disturbance had been an Elizabethan ditch—perhaps contemporary with those he had found around his outwork.

What, one might ask, suggests such a relationship?

The answer lies in the nature of the artifacts found in the trench's filling, most of them clustered toward the northern edge of square I.B.11 and comprising thirteen crucible sherds (nine of them almost certainly from the same vessel), one large Martincamp flask fragment and a lump of melted lead waste. That no domestic ceramics, animal bones or oyster shells were present clearly identifies these finds with those from the outwork whose ditch also yielded fragments from a Martincamp flask (see drawing on page 92). Because the lead, like most (if not all) of the sherds, had been disturbed and probably redeposited, one could not be certain that it was of Science Center origin. Nevertheless, lead was an important component of the assaying process, and on Frobisher's 1578 voyage, his workers carried with them one thousand pounds of it.[200]

Although the irregularly shaped lump of lead may have been undatable, another spoke for its time with unusual eloquence. The object is a merchant's seal of the kind used to identify the maker, dyer or marketer of woolen fabric and appears to be impressed with the initials HL (or JL) in relief between the standard cross-tailed 4 and XX merchant's symbol common in the Fort Raleigh period. No settler had those initials, and there is no assurance that the seal came to America attached to goods. It may, instead, have been brought along with much more old lead. Nevertheless, the HL initials represent the only contemporary English letters found and read since White's last leavers wrote CROATOAN on their palisade gate. Unfortunately, the seal was not recognized until several weeks later when project curator Audrey Noël Hume was washing the artifacts and found it loose in the bottom of a bag. With the potential to supply a date for the fort's construction, there is no knowing precisely where it lay, and in the

Field-drawn plan showing areas opened within the earthwork in 1992 with Harrington's previously excavated "early" (ditch or trench) feature stippled. *FCF.*

The excavated seal flanked by a complete example and a penny for scale. *Drawing by LNH.*

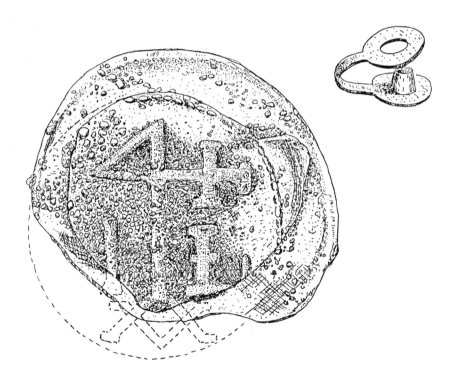

Cloth seal of lead found in the "early" trench or ditch within the reconstructed earthwork. The initials may be JL or HL. Surviving diam. ¾ inch (1.9 cm.); F.R.E.R. 41J. The diagram (*upper right*) shows how such seals were folded and clamped. *FCF.*

absence of certainty, it must be grouped with the crucible and other items from the old trench's backfill.[201]

In summation, the Virginia Company can state, not as a theory but as an artifactually and stratigraphically proven fact, that the earthwork recognized in the nineteenth century was not Ralph Lane's first built fort but postdates the commencement of assaying associated with Thomas Harriot and Joachim Gans, who were working there earlier than September 1585. Thus, with Lane's fort located elsewhere, one is left to question whether the settlement lay anywhere near the park's reconstructed earthwork. What clues can lead us to that location? What artifacts would we expect to find?

Chapter 5

THINGS THEY BROUGHT,
LEFT OR TOOK AWAY

In trying to determine what one should expect to find on a site occupied for a few years by two groups of more than one hundred people, as well as by fifteen or eighteen who were quickly burned out, the best way to begin is to determine what they needed to stay alive and to perform such tasks as would have been expected of them. For strictly archaeological purposes, one would omit such equipment, clothing and foodstuffs made or grown from organic materials that would not normally survive in the Roanoke Island ground: e.g., breeches, beans, beds, barrels, boxes, books, bagpipes and the like. The broader historical picture is less restrictive. In any case, we must remember the specific circumstances of the colonists' departure that would suggest that some objects more than others would be left behind.

Lane's people evacuated in haste, but not so precipitously that they could not pack up their most valued possessions and pile them aboard the boats that were to carry them out to Drake's fleet. One can imagine that most records, notebooks, drawings, plant samples, souvenir Indian pots and saleable pearls were packed into boxes and trunks, as were scientific instruments and any tableware of silver or silver gilt. Weapons, too, like swords and matching daggers, as well as pistols, would have been strapped on and carried out, but firearms heavier than calivers would have been abandoned. So, too, would munition-quality armor, all household goods, furniture, food, kitchenware and common tableware, agricultural and mining tools and even the lightest of artillery. Most of this material would soon be carried off by the Indians, who would have stripped the dwellings and stores of anything useful. We know, however, that they left the house structures alone—which is curious.

Arthur Barlowe's account of the first voyage had told how, twenty years earlier, Indians had come upon part of a wrecked ship "out of whose sides they drew the nayles and the spikes, and with those they made their best instruments."[202] One must speculate, therefore, that either there was so much to loot that no one bothered to salvage nails or that the houses were built almost entirely with hardwood treenails or by simpler traditional techniques.

The next arrivals, the luckless Grenville garrison, were left with supplies to last them two years and four cast-iron cannon of unspecified caliber.[203] To understand what each of these men needed to become a colonist in the New World, we can turn to guidelines reputedly compiled by Raleigh, but that continued in use into the 1630s. Victuals for a year comprised eight bushels of meal, two of peas and beans, two of oatmeal, one gallon of aqua vitae and two gallons of vinegar. To protect himself, the neophite colonial householder required "2 armors complete light, 1 long peece five foote and a halfe neere musket bore, 1 sword, 1 belt, 1 bandolier, 20 pounds of powder, 60 pound of shot or lead pistoll and Goose shott."

For a family of six, the necessary tools were listed as follows:

5 broad haws
5 narrow haws
2 broad axes
5 felling axes
2 steele hand saws
2 hand saws
1 whip saw
1 whip saw set and filed, with file and wrest
2 hammers
3 shovells
2 spades
2 augers
6 chissells
2 [?] stockell
3 gimblets
2 hatchets
2 frows to cleave pale
2 hand bills
1 grindstone
nails of all sortes
2 pickaxes

Household implements for the same specimen six-person family comprised "1 Iron pot, 1 kettle, 2 large firing pan, 1 Gridiron, 2 skillets, 1 spit, platters, dishes, spoons of wood." The inventory ends by noting, "The whole charges for 50 men will amount to a thousand pound Sterling."[204] A listing of this kind gives some hint of the quantity and variety of equipment taken over by each of John White's 1587 families. Knowing that they would have to be able to walk at least part of the way to the site of their intended "Cittie of Ralegh," it seems highly unlikely that they would have carried their domestic and agriculture tools with them but instead would have left them with the Croatoan rearguard to be shipped north when White's expected supply fleet reached Hatteras.

Ralph Lane's rather differently oriented colonists had included miners trained to search and dig for ores. Frobisher had taken a team of them to Baffin Island, and it is reasonable to assume that the Roanoke Island group, although much smaller, was comparably supplied:

120 shovels
38 spades
100 mattocks
800 baskets
10 iron crow bars of 30 lb each
10 iron sledges of 20 lb each
10 iron sledges of 10 lb each
35 iron wedges of 8 lb each
34 iron wedges of 5 lb each
30 pick axes of 8 lb each
32 small plate wedges
8 iron hoops
81 pick axes of 7.1 lb each
64 iron wedges of 5.0 lb each
30 small picks of 3.6 lb each
4 iron wedges }
24 iron plates }
1 scraper[?] } 568 lb total
36 great hammers }
3 small hammers }
12 iron crow bars of 30 lb each
24 iron wedges of 7 lb each
77 pickaxes

110 iron wedges
10 sledges
30 shovels and other miner's tools[205]

Additional equipment included twenty wheelbarrows, twenty handbarrows and three hundred hafts for pickaxes. Now, it is true that by the time Frobisher's third voyage was being fitted out, he and his backers knew that this was primarily an expedition to mine gold from Baffin Island's reluctant rocks, whereas Lane's people had no assurance that there was anything to be mined. But even so, they would almost certainly have been guided in large measure by Frobisher's experience. No doubt all the heavy iron miners' tools would have been stored where Gans could keep an eye on them and thus in the vicinity of the Science Center—where none remained to be found by archaeologists.

The only identifiable tools discovered in or near the earthwork were the axe found by Civil War treasure hunters, the sickle and auger unearthed by Harrington from the fort's ditch and the fishhook from the Science Center.

Lane's expedition was strong on soldiers, meaning that in addition to swords and daggers (which most would have carried home), they would have been equipped with sixty or more muskets, as many long and short pikes and bills, bows long and cross and fifty or sixty targets (small, round, leather-covered shields), as well as large quantities of lead and iron shot.[206] Armor, too, would have been left behind in profusion by Lane's settlers, for most soldiers would have been supplied with a cuirass (breast- and backplates) and at least a simple cabasset helmet, none of which they would have been anxious to ship out. That would not have been so of the 1587 colonists, who could have done without wheelbarrows or pickaxes but not without their arms and armor.

There is good reason to suppose that some of the dwellers in Lane's village were less able to pack than were others. While he and Drake debated, officers who "were the chiefest of the English Colony" were conferring with their opposite numbers aboard the ship *Francis* and were blown out to sea as the hurricane bore down on the fleet.[207] In the rush to be gone, it is unlikely that much attention was paid to the possessions of those who had already left and who might well be drowned. In his famed study of the "new found land," Harriot named some of the specialist equipment that he would certainly have made every effort to carry home: mathematical instruments, sea compasses, a perspective glass, spring clocks and "many other things that we had."[208] Some hint of the quality and variety of those other things is provided by the inventory of state-of-the-art technological wonders purchased for Frobisher's first Arctic voyage. Although these were needed primarily for oceanic navigational use, comparable equipment would almost certainly have been retained by Harriot for surveying and cartographic purposes:

> an Instrument of brasse named Sphera Nautica with a Case.
> a great Instrument of brase named Holometrum Geometricum with a case.
> a great instrument of brase named Horologium Universale, with a case.
> a ring of brase named Annalus Astronomicus. ·
> a littel standinge levell of brase.
> a case with smalle instrumentes for geometrie, of yron.
> an Instrument of wood, a stafe named Balistella, with a case.
> 20 Compasses of divers sortes.
> 18 hower glasses.
> a Astrolabium.[209]

Although in 1586, such expensive equipment is unlikely to have been deliberately left behind by the evacuating colonists, it is entirely possible that some items packed in boxes or trunks too big to load would have been abandoned and that pieces of them may one day be found in Indian graves or be discovered during grading on the site of what once was Roanoke Inlet and into which the passengers' boxes had been tossed by Drake's unsympathetic sailors.

Science-related objects of lesser value would almost certainly have been abandoned. The glassware was unshippable, and crucibles and ceramic flasks were not worth salvaging, nor were furnaces worth dismantling to retrieve their metal parts. Much would have been left for the Indians to haul home, and because so little remained to be found in excavations, one must assume that they did so.[210] We may deduce, too, that unlike European mobs and looters, the Indians did not smash and destroy for the pleasure of it; otherwise, more broken or burned artifacts would have found their way into the ground.

The only intact science-related object to have survived—at least long enough to be found in the mid-nineteenth century—was the sealed glass globe or vial of mercury.[211]

If the site of Grenville's garrison's burned store survives, somewhere there have to be burned objects. Because the only burned artifacts so far discovered all relate to the scientific activities, one might be prompted to conclude that Grenville's store was not located in this area. However, the building may well have measured no more than thirty by twenty feet, and many such areas remain untested south, west and north of the reconstructed earthwork. Furthermore, excavations of burned post-in-the-ground buildings in Martin's Hundred have demonstrated that because the heat from burning thatch-roofed cottages swiftly rises and as quickly cools, the archaeological evidence may be limited to the carbonizing of a single post.[212]

The question of how little or how much White's colonists left behind is umbilically entwined with the enigma of their departure. For want of any better theory, let us assume that the steps outlined earlier are correct, namely that the majority went north while a rearguard went south to Croatan Island transporting the heavy baggage to await the arrival of White's 1588 relief fleet. The latter would have retained at least one pinnace, while all the smaller boats would have carried the doomed colonists north up Currituck Sound into Back Bay. But once there, they would have been forced to continue overland into the territory of the Nansemond tribe or to venture out into the open sea. A tradition of somewhat recent origin has the colonists settling in the vicinity of Virginia Beach. As the intent was to create the "Cittie of Ralegh" at a place both readily defended and able to harbor transatlantic shipping, a site near Lynnhaven Inlet Bay makes better sense than, say, the boardwalk section of Virginia Beach. Be that as it may, recognizing that the people would need to stay together rather than advance in relays and would have expected to have to walk part of the way suggests the need to travel light. They also knew that, like Lane's people before them, they might wait in vain for White to return. Indeed, they had no assurance that he ever reached England or that his return fleet would not fall victim to weather or Spaniards.

It is fair to expect, therefore, that the settlers would be taking armor, arms and ammunition for every man; kitchen equipment for communal feeding (then called the "common kettle"); and such saws and other tools as would be needed to build houses and defenses. But much else, including nonessential niceties of life, would have been left either to be brought up aboard the fleet or to be retrieved on a return trip to Roanoke Island once the "Cittie of Ralegh" was established and its citizens secure. The fate of the colony is encapsulated in a single apocryphal sentence published some thirty-seven years later when Samuel Purchas added a note to his mammoth compendium stating that the emperor Powhatan "had bin at the murther of that Colonie: and shewed to Captain Smith a Musket barrell and a brasse Morter, and certaine peeces of Iron which had bin theirs."[213] Of these three objects, only one has the sound of an attractive souvenir: namely, the mortar. A single intact example has so far been found in Virginia. Dated 1590 and too late for Lost Colony relevance, it is probably Dutch, and small—the kind of thing an apothecary would use.[214] Brass or bell metal mortars came much larger, however. Alternatively, therefore, Powhatan's mortar was small and had indeed belonged to the Lost Colony's physician, or it was large and probably too heavy to have been carried north by the light-traveling evacuees.

Next, and probably more significant, we have the musket barrel—not a whole musket, just the barrel. If Powhatan had been present at the settlers' slaughter, he would almost certainly have been able to bring home muskets galore.

Finally, we have the "certaine peeces of Iron." If Smith had seen these relics and recognized them for what they were or had been, surely he would have said, say, "several old hinges and a mattock." The alternative is that the iron was just that—shapeless pieces or like "the many barres of Iron" that White found in 1590 within the palisades, "almost overgrown with grasse and weeds."[215] Because such bars would not have been taken north with the first exodus, one cannot escape the suspicion that like many other splinters from the True Cross, the emperor's relics were not what they were claimed to be. Were they, instead, souvenirs salvaged from the attacked and burned storehouse of 1586, or were they picked up several years later from within the settlers' abandoned Roanoke Island palisade? The latter possibility is not so outrageous when one remembers that 113 years later, John Lawson found a musket's powder horn still there, still unsalvaged. Although irrelevant to this study, it may be noted that if the massacre's souvenirs are bogus, it is more than likely that Powhatan lied to Smith when he told him that he was there.

The previously discussed enigma of John White's chests is scarcely less puzzling than the scope of Powhatan's souvenirs, but it has relevance as a description not only of the kinds of possessions he left on the island but also of the time-suggesting impact of weather upon them, as well as being further evidence of the Indians' extraordinary selectivity. One wonders, of course, what books White had elected to bring to the New World and whose covers were now missing. Although the choice was limited, there was no more uniformity in literary taste in Elizabeth's reign than there is today, and so it may be worth considering the books that Frobisher took with him on his first voyage:

a bible englishe, great volume
a new world of Andreas Thevett
englishe and frenche bookes ij small
a regiment of medina, spanishe
Sir John Mandeville, englishe[216]

This last is of more than passing interest as a testament to its time. Mandeville's *Travels* was a bestseller of its day and provided explorers heading for the Orient with exciting and inspiring accounts of the wonders of the East. It is quite reasonable, therefore, that a copy of this guide to travelers should have been in White's library along with a "bible englishe, great volume."[217] In the late sixteenth century, most books, both large and small, were bound between leather-covered boards whose corners were reinforced and decorated with embossed metal ornaments, usually with a matching central brass mount and fore edge clasps to keep the covers from yawning. It would have been these light and wearable metal ornaments that would have prompted the Indians to tear White's books apart.

Describing the artifacts that he found in the long grass, White made a point of classifying them collectively as "heavie things." Lawson, on the other hand, wrote of much lighter and smaller relics, the powder horn and "some old English Coins," the latter evidently found by someone else but there nonetheless.[218] The small artillery pieces, however, were common to both visitors. White was there in August 1590 when the grass and weeds would have been at their tallest. But this was vegetation that had grown and died through the winters of '89 and '90, providing ample opportunity for scavengers to scour and strip the site. Yet they chose not to do so, nor did they for a further century and more—which, to say the least, is odd.

We know that Indians were still coming to the island in the first years of the eighteenth century, for it was they who directed Lawson to the site. If, therefore, it was not the Indians who removed the cannon and every last trace of White's or Lane's artifacts from the earthwork, then who did? Two answers are possible: later eighteenth-century visitors or the beating waves of Albemarle Sound eroding another site unrelated to the earthwork.

Turning now from artifacts known or suggested only through the contemporary narratives and inventories, one must consider the testimony of the sherds actually found on the Fort Raleigh site. Their limited range and the inferences to be drawn therefrom are discussed below, and in the great scheme of things, the number of separate crucibles or Martincamp flasks that can be identified from the fragments is of little consequence. They

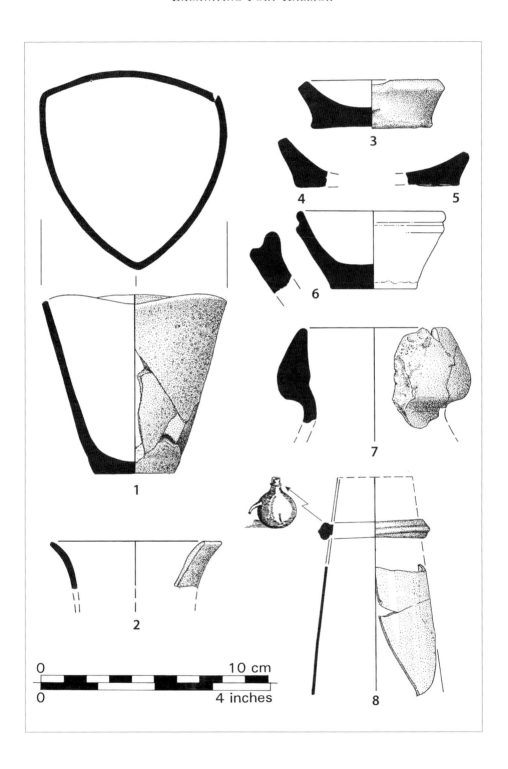

represent only a fraction—indeed, an unknown fraction, of those that would have been used during the eight months of Gans's presence. What do matter, however, are the tiny beads of cuprous metal imbedded in the scoria and flux attached to the inner faces of some of the sherds. Seven prills (or pellets) were taken from four crucibles by Drs. Robert M. Ehrenreich and Petar Glumac and found to be primarily copper with occasional trace elements of silver. Because antimony was found only in the large cuprous lump from the earthwork's ditch, they concluded that this specimen alone had been assayed in the hope of extracting gold. The samples from the crucibles also contained tin and zinc, and in one instance, a piece of iron scale akin to the many flakes found in a ten-foot area of the Science Center was found attached to a sherd by the copper-based residue. Robert Ehrenreich concluded that was being deliberately added and that the metallurgical residues were the result of assaying.[219]

Opposite: 1. Crucible, granular-surfaced gray ware, triangular mouth and flat base. Base not joining but believed to be the same vessel; height approx. 4 in. (10.16 cm.), base diam.: 1³/₈ in. (3.54 cm.). Unused. F.R.E.R. 2A and 8G 371. One sherd from workshop floor (8G), ten joining fragments from Harrington's 1965 backfill (2A).
2. Crucible, refined granular-surfaced gray ware, a thin and everted mouth sherd, probably from a round-mouthed vessel of beaker form. Estimated mouth diam. 3 in. (7.62 cm.). No evidence of use. F.R.E.R. 48A.
3. Cupel, heavily micaceous, pinkish buff ware with thin surface slip of the same clay, very crudely made with slightly everted lip and very shallow saucer-like interior. Diam. 2½ in. (6.35 cm.), ht. ¾ in. (1.90 cm.) No evidence of use. F.R.E.R. 31B no. 81 and 2A.
4. Cupel, ware, shape and size as above. No evidence of use. F.R.E.R .8G no. 37.
5. Cupel, same micaceous ware as nos. 3 and 4, shallower, ht. ⁹/₁₆ in. (1.4 cm.). Clay flakes on base appear to be fabric impressed. No evidence of interior use. F.R.E.R. 2A.
6. Cupel, rim sherd of unusual form, having an expanded wall below the exterior lip, a characteristic matched by smaller sixteenth-century examples found in Austria, one of which is shown to the right, its base diam. 1½ in (Pittioni, *Zwei Weitere Probierschlächen*, figs. 2–4). (3.81 cm.). The Fort Raleigh fragment is heavily vitrified from use (so heavily vitrified is this fragment that one cannot be sure that it does not come from the neck of an Iberian jar akin to no. 7.). F.R.E.R. 40E.
7. Jar neck, Iberian, a sandy buff ware, the exterior rim markedly undercut and the neck unusually thin. The fragments of this jar are vitrified; it appears to have broken while mouth down in the furnace. Estimated max. rim diam. 2.91 in. (7.4 cm.) F.R.E.R. 40D no. 62 and Harrington 1965 no. 26. This jar neck belongs to the same class as Harrington's specimen from the fort ditch (*Cittie of Raleigh*, 22, fig. 20). The rim form belongs to Goggin's "Middle Style," circa 1580–1800, but the dating in this pioneering work has since been found to be too loose to be useful (Goggin, *Spanish Olive Jar*, 13, fig. 5, forms A and D).
8. Retort, neck fragment and string rim, pale green forest glass, probably German (with vessel form of 1574). Estimated mouth diam. ¹¹/₄ in. (3.17 cm.) Neck fragments F.R.E.R. 31B and 40G no. 34; string rim 39B.
Ceramics and glass from the Science Center. Deposition date for all: September 1585 to June 1586. *Drawn by JM.*

In 1980, the Austrian archaeologist Dr. Rudolph Werner Soukup discovered debris from a comparable assaying effort at Gut Oberstockstall in Lower Austria, the deposit given a *terminus post quem* of 1549 by the inclusion of a dated butter mold. He described finding many melting pots, the majority of them "crucibles with circular bases and triangular-shaped openings: approximately 280 pieces." The smallest crucible had a height of only 1.6 cm and the tallest 22 cm. Dr. Soukup stated that they fell into five sizes and were made from "gray clay heavily leaned with graphite." Unlike the Roanoke examples, none of which are marked, his larger specimens were impressed on their bases with a single or double *T* within a shield of arms. Another smaller type carried the initials I.E. over a vine and two triangles.[220]

The Science Center crucible fragments numbered 119, of which 27 came from within the fort. Unfortunately, most were small, and only one could be partially pieced together, although it was evident that those in the Science Center area came from at least six vessels. All were rough-surfaced and gray in color, some exhibiting a thin reddish band at the lip. Similar bands are found on the lips of unused and early eighteenth-century examples found in Williamsburg and also on an unidentified shipwreck site in Bermuda and are thought to be a deliberately applied edging of iron oxide.[221] All the examples from Fort Raleigh are of the triangular variety, and most seem to have been about three inches in height. The shape is of considerable antiquity and was still in use in Williamsburg in the third quarter of the eighteenth century.[222]

Although considerably older, the art of making crucibles described in *De Diversis Artibus* by the Benedictine monk Theophilis had probably changed little since the end of the twelfth century:

> *Take fragments of old vessels in which copper or bronze have been previously melted and break them up small over a stone. Then take the clay from which pots are made, and of which there are two kinds—one white, the other grey. (Of these, the white is useful for* [crucibles used when] *coloring gold, and the other for making these vessels.) When you have ground it for a very long time, you mix this raw clay with the other…in the following proportion. Take any small container and fill it twice with the raw clay and three times with the fired substance so that two parts are raw and a third fired. Put them together in a large vessel, pour on warm water, and vigorously knead with hammers and the hands until the mixture becomes completely sticky. Then take a round piece of wood, cut it to the size which you want the vessel to be in accordance with the capacity of the kiln, and on it mold your crucible. When it is shaped, you cover it round with dry*

ashes and place it near the fire, as it is, until dry. When they have been carefully dried, put in the kiln three, four, or five—as many as the kiln can take—and surround them with coals.[223]

To German metallurgists like Joachim Gans, the principal types of crucibles were known as *Catilli triangularis* and *Catilli cinereus*, the latter known in English as cupels, small and shallow cups or dishes used to separate precious metals from lead. Fragments of two examples were found on the Science Center floor, one of them almost complete.[224] In addition, the finds include a thick, heavily vitrified and externally stepped rim sherd from the same ware as the crucibles and very closely paralleled by a cupel found in the Austrian Tirol in a context of the second half of the sixteenth century.[225] It is possible that this very distinctive and yet unusual form may be read as evidence that Gans had taken Germanic equipment with him to Roanoke Island.[226]

Greater in sherd count (136) though almost certainly fewer in vessel number than crucibles were sherds of gray Martincamp flasks of the type often described as costrels because many were cased in straw or osier and carried as water bottles.[227] The Fort Raleigh examples, however, were almost certainly used as retorts or distilling receivers, the former identified by the presence of heated deposits on the interior faces of some fifteen sherds. The only restorable example yet found at the Fort Raleigh site was that found by Harrington in 1965 (see photograph on page 85), but there is no record of any deposit being found inside it.[228]

Describing the finds from Gut Oberstockstall, Dr. Soukup reported that "microphase x-ray structure analysis of the residue on the inner walls of a large ceramic retort [revealed] several antimony alloys." Another base fragment was found to contain hematite, magnetite and copper oxide. These he assumed to be the distillation residues from the making of sulfuric acid.[229]

The flasks are of unusual construction, being made as two hemispherical bowls luted together to create the globular body shape. Necks were turned separately and set into a hole cut into the side of the ball at a point along the line of the lute. Flasks of this general type are now known to fall into three categories and divided by color into three subtypes that are assigned different dates, beginning with an off-white to buff variety that may have been in production as early as the late fifteenth century and that went on into the mid-sixteenth century. At Fort Raleigh these are represented by three sherds from the Science Center site, suggesting a great longevity.[230] Type II (stoneware) is of the same shape and construction and a gray to purplish-

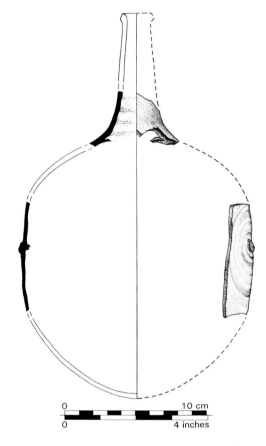

0 ⊣⊢ 10 cm
0 ⊣⊢ 4 inches

Left: Flask or costrel of Martincamp gray to pinkish stoneware; neck and side nipple fragments are here used as representative of 136 sherds recovered during the 1991–92 excavations. Although these diagnostic sherds were among thirty-two recovered from Harrington's backfill (F.R.E.R. 2A), other, smaller pieces were found in the undisturbed Science Center context. Deposition date: 1585–86. *Drawing by JM.*

Below: Polychrome-decorated pharmaceutical jars of Anglo-Netherlandish tin-glazed earthenware comparable in size and character to sherds found on the Science Center site. Tallest 3⅜ inches (8.6 cm). Palette of underglaze blue, orange and purple. *FCF.*

red in color due to variations in the kiln's essentially reducing atmosphere. Dating for this gray type is loose and is thought to span most, if not all, of the sixteenth century. Clearly, it was common in 1585. Type III (earthenware) is usually smaller and fired in an oxidizing atmosphere and therefore red in color. Examples of this have been found at Jamestown and on other Virginia sites of the seventeenth century.[231] All three flask varieties have been found near Martincamp, which lies between Dieppe and Beauvais in Northern France, and so generally are ascribed to that source.[232]

Fragments of tin-glazed earthenware were found both by Harrington and by Ehrenhard, most of them in the latter's 1983 excavation on the Science Center site, when they were thought to be Spanish. The largest fragments were found in 1950 and "recovered from loose earth when shaping up parapet"—further evidence of the scientific activity having extended beneath the later fort (see drawing on page 92).[233] Eighteen additional sherds from the 1991–92 excavations were all very small and very burned, save for one rim sherd discovered in Harrington's outwork backfill. The size and condition of the rest of the fragments was such that only four could be attributed to any particular shape, and these all came from pharmaceutical drug jars of the size and polychrome type illustrated here. Tin-glazed earthenware (later generically called delftware) had been made in England by emigrant Netherlandish potters from Antwerp in 1567 who settled first at Norwich and moved to Aldgate in London four years later. Waster fragments of small galley pots, as they were then called, have been found in excavations at the junction of Ber Street and Thorn Lane in Norwich.[234] After the Antwerp potters' move to London, similarly painted pots continued to be made there through the first half of the seventeenth century. Consequently, there is no reason to preclude the Roanoke pots from being of English origin. But with that said, one must remember that identical pots were also being made in the Netherlands, sometimes using clays imported from England.

In 1609 a hurricane blew the ship *Sea Venture* onto a Bermudian reef, where she stuck fast and provided her crew and passengers with time to salvage whatever was necessary to build two new ships and sail on to Virginia. Not needed or not found were several tall jars manufactured in North Devon and generally known to have transported butter, fish and similar commodities. When recovered from the wreck in 1978, they were the earliest known examples of a ware and vessel type that would be common in the American colonies through the first third of the seventeenth century.[235] Eight sherds, probably all from the same jar, have since been found on and around the Science Center floor, making 1585 the earliest confirmed date for this West

Fort Raleigh project curator Audrey Noël Hume and diving archaeologist J. Wingood examining North Devon baluster jars from the wreck of the *Sea Venture* that parallel fragments from the Science Center site. *FCF.*

of England ware. Internally lead-glazed, such jars could have been used for any number of purposes in the Harriot-Gans assay shop, but the recovered fragments may well have come from a jar used, as contemporary port records' nomenclature would have it, as a butter pot. Agricola in his monumental *De Re Metallica* (1555) illustrated an assayer's furnace and in front of it a hooded man holding a large jar, its caption explaining: "The foreman when hungry eats butter, that the poison which the crucible exhales may not harm him, for this is a special remedy against the poison."[236] The "litharge" in the print refers to lead monoxide (PbO), a yellowish or reddish, odorless, heavy, earthy, water-insoluble, poisonous residue from silver extraction. There is, of course, no proving that Gans and his workers sat around in their laboratory eating butter, yet it is hard to dismiss the provisioning jars' presence as purely coincidental.

Of the European artifacts, only the glass remains to be discussed, and alas, there is not a great deal to say of it—beyond the significant fact that the largest fragments come from a vessel specifically identifiable as an item of assayers' glassware, namely part of the neck and string rim (see no. 8 in illustration on page 132) from one described in 1574 as "a receiver used in fractional distillation."[237] Twenty-five glass fragments were recovered, most

A—FURNACE. B—STICKS OF WOOD. C—LITHARGE. D—PLATE. E—THE FOREMAN WHEN HUNGRY EATS BUTTER, THAT THE POISON WHICH THE CRUCIBLE EXHALES MAY NOT HARM HIM, FOR THIS IS A SPECIAL REMEDY AGAINST THAT POISON.

Agricola's 1556 illustration from *De Re Metallica* showing a worker eating butter from a jar as a remedy against the poisonous fumes from a metalworking furnace. *Public domain.*

of them tiny slivers and fingernail-sized pieces and all (save for the previously discussed neck) too small for vessel identification. (See in situ glass shards in photograph on page 111.)

Although, because of its fragility, the glass might be assumed to be of English manufacture, there is evidence pointing to its importation from Germany. A 1621 petition against the English glass monopolist Sir Robert Mansell claimed that "chimicall glasses, as retorte heades and bodies, boulte heades and other like used for extractions distillacion and other Chimicall and Physical uses" had been imported from Germany before James I granted Mansell his monopoly and that they were better and cheaper. English port records show that in 1587–88, one hundred glass

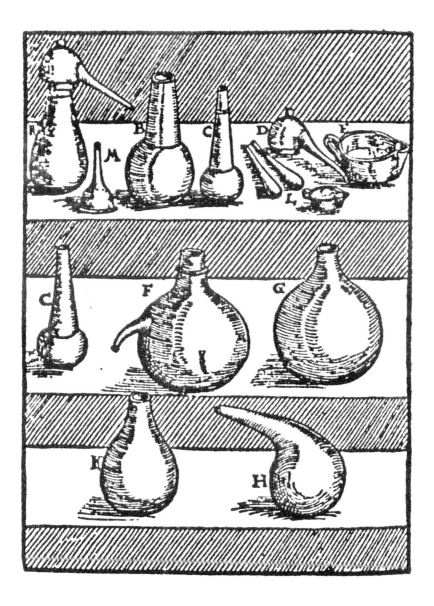

Assayer's chemical glassware as illustrated by Lazarus Ercker in his *Treatise on Ores and Assaying* that was published in 1574 in Prague in the German language. The central spouted vessel (F) is identified as a "receiver used in fractional distillation." Its neck matches fragments from the Science Center site. *Image from https://www.martayanlan.com/ pages/books/2295/lazarus-ercker/aula-subterranea-domina-dominantium-subdita-subditorum-das-ist- untererdische-hofhaltung-ohne.*

stills were imported from Dortmund and two hundred "stilling glasses" from Emden.[238] Thus, with German imports preferred by the users and user Gans being from Prague, one couples that with the illustration of comparable glassware from the pages of the German Lazarus Ercker's 1574 Prague-published treatise,[239] and a German *waldglas* factory becomes the likely source for the Fort Raleigh glassware.

Two more artifact categories are European in origin and relate directly to the Science Center operation: namely, 58 flint chips and 106 iron scales. The latter, as previously noted, were concentrated within a single ten-foot square and were scattered across a stratum of gray and very sandy soil. It remains only to be noted that the concentration points either to the place where the iron was used or where it was stored.[240] The 58 flint chips were more widely distributed, but even these were found in a radius of only fifteen feet. Most were white, apparently as the result of calcination, but a few were black and akin to English nodules from the south coastal chalk, while others exhibit the honey color of French flint. English and European flint have been found on the Frobisher expeditions' sites, but usually amid coal dumps; they are thought to have become mixed with it when both served as ballast.[241]

The Fort Raleigh examples, however, seem to have been deliberately pulverized and to have been used for an as-yet-to-be-determined purpose. Ground flint has long been used as a source of silica in the manufacture of ceramic glazes and in glassmaking (flint glass). It is possible that ground flint and iron scales were used in the making of a cementing lute for packing a joint (as in laboratory apparatus) or in coating a porous surface to make it impervious to gas or liquid. Two assumptions can reasonably be made: (1) that chips were pulverized from flints of at least two varieties and (2) that they were brought to Roanoke Island for a purpose associated with Science Center activities.

European objects were not the only ceramics unearthed at Fort Raleigh. The aboriginal artifacts were studied by Dr. David Phelps of the Department of Anthropology, East Carolina University, and his observations are incorporated below. While there had been Indian occupation and use of the island long before the arrival of the English and for more than a century after they left, nothing has been found in the immediate vicinity of the Science Center or the reconstructed earthwork for which a colonial explanation is impossible. The discovery of a shattered Indian bowl of Mangoak origin on the Science Center floor was unequivocal proof that the English had used Indian vessels in their experimental work.[242] The bowl had been greatly heated to the point of flaking and was found with fine

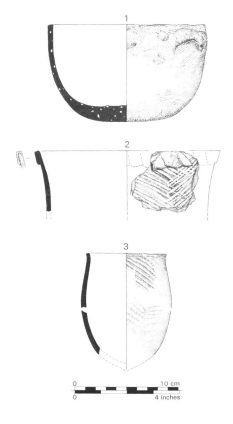

0   10 cm
0   4 inches

Left: Examples of aboriginal pottery from the 1991–92 excavations. (1) Pebble-tempered bowl possibly used as a cucurbit and found on the Science Center floor; it is thought to be Cashie ware traded into the coastal area from the Mangoaks (F.R.E.R. 8D, 8G.31B et al); (2) An unusual folded and impressed rim from a Colington ware bowl recovered from the F.R.E.R. A2 backfill; and (3) A Colington ware beaker F.R.E.R. 53A and 55B) found in the "early" trench or ditch within the earthwork. *Drawing by JM.*

Below: The Cashie ware bowl from the Science Center floor. *FCF.*

Opposite: Algonquian tobacco pipe found by J.C. Harrington in the earthwork's ditch (no. 98). *Photo by Block.*

142

sand concreted around it, suggesting that it had served as a sand-bedded cucurbit in the distilling process.[243]

A sherd unique to the site belonged to the shell-tempered Colington series and was characterized by a slightly flaring rim, thickened by an applied and finger-impressed band.[244] This came from backfill in the area of Harrington's outwork, and one may safely assume that it had seen English service in the Science Center area. A third Indian vessel was found in the ditch or trench within the fort partially excavated by Harrington in 1950.[245] This is of significance in that it is a smaller version of the most complete pot that he found at the bottom of the earthwork's ditch, suggesting that both came from the same source and were used at the same time by the English and probably for the same purpose.[246]

Perhaps most evocative of the Indian artifacts were the few fragments of tobacco pipes found in the Science Center area, one of them a thick mouthpiece recovered from the workshop floor after having fallen from English—or maybe German—lips.[247] Tradition has it that tobacco was first introduced into England by Sir Walter Raleigh (along with the potato) and brought there by one of his returning captains. The British antiquary the Reverend A. Hume, in an 1863 essay on tobacco pipes, was unusually cautious:

> *It is certain that the use of American tobacco in this country commenced in the reign of Queen Elizabeth, about 1585, that it spread with great rapidity, and attracted much attention….Few assert that the smoking-tube (used in connection with some substance) was then manufactured for the first time; the argument is that from that date it came in to extensive use, and in the forms with which we are familiar. There is thus both negative and positive evidence…that smoking-tubes or pipes were known in the British islands before the time of Elizabeth.*[248]

Although it is highly likely that the joys of tobacco reached the English court through diplomatic contacts with Spain much earlier in the sixteenth century, the white clay tobacco pipe is first documented archaeologically in

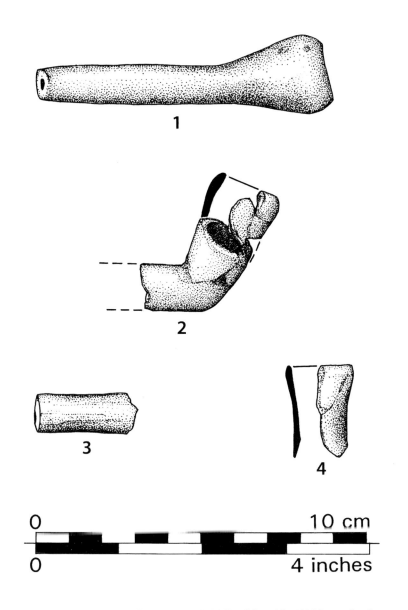

Tobacco artifacts: (1) Found by J.C. Harrington); (2) Bowl found in 1992 immediately west of the earthwork (F.R.E.R. 10K); (3) Mouthpiece from the Science Center floor (F.R.E.R.31B no. 86); (4) Bowl sherd from an adjacent 1585–86 layer (F.R.E.R. 8E). *Drawn by JM.*

England in the last years of Elizabeth's reign; the Reverend Hume's 1585 date may well be right—if the first North Carolinian samples of both weed and pipe were taken back by Grenville in the fall of that year. It is possible, of course, that it was left to Harriot to peddle the product, for it was he who would write that

> *we ourselves during the time we were there used to suck it after their* [the Indian] *maner, as also since our returne, & have found manie rare and wonderful experiments of the vertues thereof; of which the relation woulde require a volume by itselfe: the use of it by so manie of late, men & women of great calling as else, and some learned Phisitions also, is sufficient witnes.*[249]

Unfortunately, Thomas Harriot was wrong. His tobacco smoking proved to have little medical use. Instead, cancer led to years of suffering and his death in 1621. That smoking went on in the Science Center is evident enough, but unfortunately, the only close-to-complete Indian pipe so far discovered is the one found by Harrington in the fort ditch.[250] A badly crushed bowl with a fragment of its stem was found in 1992 in a square close to the fort entrance.[251]

Metal artifacts were few, and those that survived were in poor condition, the most interesting of them the previously mentioned fishhook. Unfortunately, it was broken in excavation, and the top of the shaft was not retrieved. Consequently, there is no telling whether it terminated in an eye or simply in an expansion of the shaft.[252] One can only speculate how it came to be in the Science Center area, but it is possible that, attached to a piece of line, it served as a suspension hook within the workshop. Also found in the Science Center floor context were nine nails, four of them small flat-headed tacks with an average length of 1.4 cm or 9/16". One was rusted to the tip of a 2.7 cm nail, suggesting that these were new nails inadvertently dropped together onto the floor—were it not for the fact that the larger of the two is bent and appears to have been drawn from its wood (no. 5 in illustration opposite). The presence of such small tacks remains yet

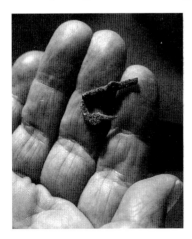

Fishhook, as excavated. *Photo by LNH.*

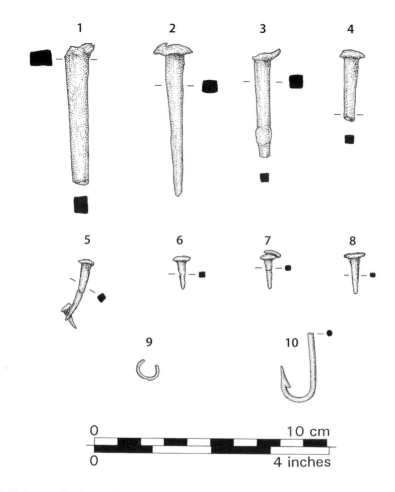

1. Nail, wrought, incomplete, surviving length 2¼ in. (5.71 cm.) F.R.E.R. 12C.
2. Nail, wrought, head flat and hammered, tip missing. Surviving length 2½ in. (6.35 cm) F.R.E.R. 8D no. 16.
3. Nail, wrought, incomplete, surviving length 1⅝ in. (4.3 cm). F.R.E.R. 8D no. 12.
4. Nail, wrought, incomplete, head slightly elevated, possibly rose-head type. Surviving length ¹¹/₈ in. (3 cm) F.R.E.R.8D no. 10.
5. Nail, wrought, with almost flat head; flat-headed tack attached. Nail length, 1 inch (2.8 cm), tack length ⅜ in. (9 mm). F.R.E.R. 12C no. 7.
6. Tack, wrought, flat-headed; length ½ inch (1.27 cm) F.R.E.R. 8F.
7. Tack, wrought, flat-headed, with head of another attached. Length ⁹/₁₆ in. (1.4 cm) F.R.E.R. 31B.
8. Tack, wrought, larger flat head than the above. Length ⅝ in. (1.5 cm). F.R.E.R. 8F.
9. Ring, round-sectioned copper alloy wire, similar in size to rings of mail, but missing the flattened ends and rivet to prove it. Width ⁷/₁₆ in. (1.1 cm). F.R.E.R. 31B no. 79.
10. Fishhook, wrought, triangular barb, top of square-sectioned shaft missing. Surviving length 1⅛ in. (2.8 cm) F.R.E.R. 8D. The hook has since disintegrated while in storage at the NPS. Southeastern Archaeological Center in Tallahassee.
Metal artifacts. Deposition date for all: September 1585 to June 1586. All ferrous unless otherwise stated. *Drawn by JM.*

Pearlware brown transfer-printed and polychrome dappled saucer whose central ornament recalls the Peace of Amiens of 1802. *Left*: A rim sherd found east of J.C. Harrington's charcoal pit demonstrates an identical decoration. *Photo by LNH.*

another of Fort Raleigh's lesser unexplained surprises.[253] Two of these tacks had lain together and clearly were dropped where they lay rather than having come from now vanished wood (no. 7 in illustration opposite).

Only one copper-alloy artifact was found: namely, a small wire ring that, had it been complete, might have been found to come from the decorative brass edging of a garment of mail. In its present state, however, one can say no more than it was found on the workshop floor (no. 9 in illustration opposite).

Finally, for the record, mention must again be made of the three small late-eighteenth-to-nineteenth-century potsherds found in the northwest corner of area IV.A.6 while clearing to reexamine Harrington's charcoal pit. They comprise a rim sherd from a small creamware plate (probably of the Royal Pattern), a wall fragment from an underglaze blue-painted creamware mug or can and a rim sherd from a brown transfer-printed saucer or bowl whose pattern matches those of several pearlware services made to commemorate the Peace of Amiens in 1802.[254] Another late brown stoneware potsherd was found on a subsequent visit to the site, lying in disturbed soil beside the concrete walkway some fifty feet distant. Together these small and undistinguished sherds carry the archaeological story of the Fort Raleigh National Historic Site across the turn of the nineteenth century and to the time when members of the Etheridge family were masters of the northern extremity of Roanoke Island.

Chapter 6

THE FORT RALEIGH EARTHWORK

Evidence and Interpretations

The bones of the historical evidence have been presented on earlier pages and are limited to Pedro Diaz's secondhand and later assertion that Ralph Lane's defenses had been no more than "a wooden fort of little strength." All else is speculation based on Lane's previous military experience, on his intention to erect earthwork sconces and on John White's rendering of a sandcastle defense system that Lane built on the Puerto Rican shore. From there, one turns to the testament of seventeenth- and eighteenth-century travelers, none of whom describe an earthwork, only a "ruin" of unspecified construction. Not until 1860 and Edward C. Bruce's report of his visit does anyone specifically describe the site as entrenched—although as early as President Monroe's visit of April 1819, that could be implied. Bruce's description was quickly followed by that of Zouave Charles Johnson, who provided the first known drawing of an earthwork. Thereafter, no one doubted that the entrenchments at the island's north end were, indeed, *the* earthwork—the "Newe Forte in Verginia" built by Ralph Lane in September 1585. This conclusion persisted through Harrington's excavations, enabling him to fit most of what he found within that interpretation.

OTHER POSSIBILITIES

In many an excavation, the archaeologist is charged with finding something that is desired by the sponsor, and in the absence of evidence to the contrary, one has every reason to draw helpfully constructive conclusions. In the present instance, however, a negative assumption was to be the catalyst for the 1991–93 excavations. The intent was to prove or disprove the proposition that J.C. Harrington's outwork predated the fortification visited by President Monroe and later visitors and that the former had served Thomas Harriot and Joachim Gans as at least part of their scientific research operation. That thesis was proved beyond all doubt, but having been so, it raised serious questions about when the dirt fort was constructed and where the Lane and White settlement had stood.

In his 1962 report, Harrington forthrightly addressed these problems:

> *Having confirmed the traditional fort site, the next step was to locate the habitation area, believed from the records to have been set apart from the fort. Discovery of the break in the fort ditch, interpreted as the major entrance to the fort, suggested that the settlement would likely be found to the west, and it was in this direction that most of the exploratory trenches were dug.*[255]

We now know, of course, that Harrington had not confirmed the site of Lane's fort, and therefore its westerly facing entrance was a bogus pointer. Nevertheless, and coincidentally, there was concentrated Lane-period activity in that direction. Here was a lesson not readily accepted by many an archaeologist, namely that trenching or shovel-testing holes can cross or straddle features of major importance without revealing them. Such was the case with Harrington's Trench P that passed through the center of the Science Center area, yielding at least one Gans-related clue along the way.[256]

Harrington went on to discuss alternative Elizabethan locations for the Lane and White settlement and admitted that were it not for having proven that the earthwork was Lane's fort, serious consideration would still need to be given to the proposition that the settlement had been located at or near the modern Mother Vineyard.[257] He was responding to a long-held belief by local historians that the Park Service had reconstructed on the wrong site and that the real Lost Colony site lay further to the east and closer to the island's principal inlet, Shallow Bag Bay, one arguably capable of having provided the best shelter for the colonists' boats.[258]

Proving that the settlement did not lie immediately west of the fort and failing to find any other evidence of its existence does not automatically thrust the three-mile-distant Mother Vineyard site into the spotlight. On the contrary, Phillip Evans's discovery of the two-barrel wells offshore north of the earthwork site strongly suggests that it was there the village had stood.

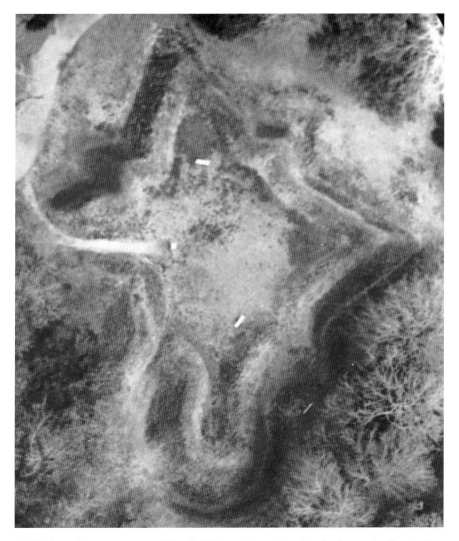

Aerial view of the reconstructed Fort Raleigh earthwork showing the "magazine" projection at bottom. View from the South. *Photo by Dave Doody.*

With that said, and although the wells are of the right period, one must allow that there is no proof that they were not located near a landing place, as has been suggested, rather than being the sole remains of the settlement.[259]

Equally problematical is the precise date of the original earthwork. Too small to shelter either the Lane or the White expedition colonists, and with its entrance pointing in a direction wherein no trace of the village has been found, the fort turns its back, as it were, on the settlement site suggested by the wells. In short, the earthwork fits comfortably into no archaeological or historical scenario. As reconstructed, and in the absence of a capping palisaded breastwork, the structure much more closely resembles an artillery emplacement than even a retreat for a handful of colonists. If correctly rebuilt—and one must remember that in spite of Park Service turfing, its contours have softened since 1950—the construction appears to be designed to mount two pieces of artillery, one aiming north and the other east. A larger projection faces south and is of an entirely different shape. This is, however, consistent with a defense for a powder magazine, providing that it had at its throat a separate mound or palisade to serve as a blast wall should an enemy shell or fire arrow alight within it. Being of lesser width and height than the original rampart and firing step, such an ancillary feature could long since have eroded away or been flattened by early preservationists who did not recognize it for what it had been.

If the earthwork was indeed an artillery emplacement, one must next consider against whom it was intended. Furthermore, no matter who the enemy or when its date, the guns' handlers would be prevented from sighting on a seaborne assailant due to the presence of the dunes that lay between them and the sound. That condition apparently existed as long ago as 1862, when a Civil War map showed a dune line in front of the site and woods to its west (see map on page 62).[260] It cannot as yet (if ever) be determined how much land has been lost since that date and whether the present dune line is the same one drawn by the 1862 cartographer. If, however, the dunes are a valid factor, one must also question what impact they or their predecessors would have had on the earthwork's sight lines at an earlier time.

Even if one assumes that the barrel wells identify the location of the Lane/White settlement, there is no knowing whether they mark its rear or its center—or if there were more now-vanished wells. Therefore, they are of no significance to the village plan. If the settlement followed the established Irish bawn format, it is likely to have been rectangular, and therefore, if laid out at a right angle to the shore, guns mounted within the earthwork could have ranged along its flanks. It must be said, however, that the Irish parallels were inland, whereas most shore-hugging fishing villages in the West of England stretched in a thin line parallel to the strand.[261]

If the earthwork was built on top of the Science Center's operation, which must have continued at least until Lane returned from his March exploration, it is safe to conclude that it did not exist when he departed with Drake in June. If the defense was built for the benefit of Grenville's men, one can reason that it would have been located to best protect them from the

Indians rather than to defend the abandoned village. That leaves only the 1587 colonizing effort. If, as we know, those people were of a mind to have the village "very strongly enclosed with a high palisado of great trees, with cortynes and flankers very Fort-like" wherein to mount their artillery, one can question why they also needed an artillery-housing sconce behind the village or even that they built it to serve until the palisades were complete.[262]

There remains another somewhat likely possibility, namely that the wells belonged not to the village but to a secondary landing below the Harriot-Gans complex and that with the latter abandoned, White's settlers built the sconce in the previously cleared area to protect the landing. That, of course, presupposes that the palisaded village was located at a considerable distance from the Science Center site—perhaps as far away as Mother Vineyard. The flaw in this reasoning is immediately apparent. With the scientific component being of paramount importance to Raleigh's first settling venture, it is hardly likely that it would have been sited at an indefensible distance from the rest of the company.

These, then, are the Raleigh era options, none of them very persuasive. We turn now to the later candidates, mindful always that if the earthwork was of Elizabethan origin, the island had not one but two forts at its northern end: the soft-contoured sconce and the fortified village from which the houses had been removed, leaving only the outer fortlike wall. Lane's fort, we remember, had been "rased down" by the time White arrived on July 23, 1587. Surprisingly, therefore, no subsequent visitor mentioned seeing two forts, only the ruins of one—one in which John Lawson found military material including, it seems, two pieces of small artillery of the kind intended for short-range and even wall-mounted defense. It is highly unlikely that such small ordnance would have been carriage-mounted in the earthwork, where to be of much use, a gun of saker bore would have been needed to do any damage to an approaching invader. On the other hand, the kinds of ordnance found within the fort by Lawson could well have been mounted in the 1587 flankers to enfilade the curtains. The similarity between the artillery seen by Lawson and that reported by White in 1590 leaves no doubt that they were viewing the same fortification. That it was not the Science Center capping earthwork seems equally certain, thus leaving the question: was the latter away in the woods or the dunes and therefore neither visited nor remembered?

Chapter 7

THE FUTURE OF THE PAST

In summarizing what we know to have existed on the Fort Raleigh National Historic Site and suggesting what the future may hold for it, one is very cognizant of the fact that the single question everyone wants answered is: What happened to the Lost Colony? Anything less is too little. Written large in the credit column, however, is the realization that the park now has a firmly documented archaeological feature: namely, the workplace of Thomas Harriot and Joachim Gans from September 1585 to June 1586. This knowledge not only frees the fort from the indefensible claim that it was built by Ralph Lane as his haven for one hundred and more settlers but also enables interpreters to point to the precise spot where Britain's premier scientist of his day and the first Jewish researcher to work in English-speaking America, together assessed the "new found land's" commercial potential. Their conclusions were destined to shape American history from that day to this. No other archaeological site or national park can make such a claim.

Unlike the outline of the earthwork, which could be traced out and reconstructed with some assurance, the Science Center has as yet offered only one defined structure, that found by Harrington in 1965 and called the outwork. Thirty years and three excavations later, no one is able or prepared to describe with certainty either its elevation or its purpose. It could have been a log-walled shed or even a watchtower high enough to maintain visual contact with a village some considerable distance away. But based on Harrington's accumulated evidence and the science-

Fig. 68. The Science Center complex as excavated in 1992. View from the southwest. *FCF*.

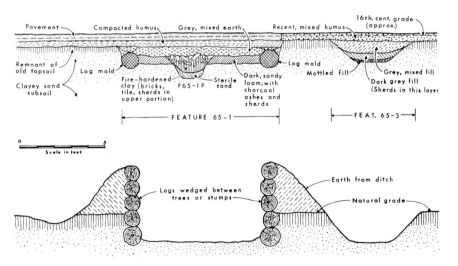

J.C. Harrington's profile and suggested interpretation of his outwork structure. *Public domain*.

related knowledge we now have, another interpretation seems reasonable. Harrington was convinced that he found traces of horizontal logs around the four trees/posts of his structure and postulated that a berm had been thrown up outside or behind them. He found much charcoal inside the structure and brickbats and small fragments in the pits, as well as clay mortar. In the largest of the pits, he found the neck of a Martincamp flask. Put all this together, and one comes up with a carport-like shed with a slightly sunken floor and perhaps breast-high log walls to control drafts and allow smoke to escape from one or more brick-built furnaces within the structure, furnaces that could as well be constructed on an iron-plate-covered table as on the ground or over an ash pit.

In his *De Re Metallica*, Agricola used two illustrations that closely parallel Harrington's findings. The latter's published report shows the interior of his structure sunk about eighteen inches below the sixteenth-century grade and conjectural log walls rising to a height of about four feet. Harrington interpreted no roof, but without it, the vertical posts would be unnecessary. A "mineralman" seated behind the log walls would be protected from sand blown at ground level and would be able to operate much as one does today at a computer table—and it is this relationship that Agricola shows in his illustrations.[263] The height of the vertical board fencing drawn there that seems to hold back rising ground parallels the log-and-berm walling postulated by Harrington. On that evidence, therefore, this writer concludes that Harrington's outwork was a partially log-walled shed wherein some of the assay-related scientific research of Gans and/or Harriot was performed. Unfortunately, even if the Science Center open-shed interpretation is close to the mark, neither past nor future archaeology is likely to enable this historic ground to be portrayed by anything more visual than a historic marker and the eloquence of the Park Service's interpreters.

It is true that the settlement site's location has been narrowed as a result of the 1991–93 excavations to the extent of demonstrating that it lies or lay somewhere other than in the immediate vicinity of the earthwork.[264] Unfortunately, negative evidence is the least desirable kind, for in this instance, it provides no hint as to the direction to be taken by future seekers after the birthplace of Virginia Dare.

In spite of the damage done by modern site improvements, there is still much ground between Harrington's charcoal pit and his outwork that may yield further information regarding the scope of the assayers' work. No well has been found that provided Harriot and Gans with their essential supply of fresh water, and if Harriot's house was anywhere near his workplace, its

ROUND ASSAY FURNACE.

RECTANGULAR ASSAY FURNACE.

Agricola's 1556 illustrations of assayers seated at bench-supported furnaces with low wooden walls that serve as a windscreen behind them. *Public domain.*

postholes should lie somewhere under those yards that remain unexplored to south, west or, more probably, north of the Science Center complex.

If the discovered well shafts were but two of several, the sub-bottom search for others could help to define the shape and size of the village. Alternatively, if the high ground sloped down to a boat landing, the bottoms of its piles may remain in the silt further offshore. So, too, might heavy artifacts, although it is likely that most of the settlement's trash would have been carried away by the current that skirts the island.

It may be said in summation that although Sir Walter Raleigh's ill-starred settlement site is still tantalizingly lost, much yet remains to be done archaeologically in the vicinity of the place where America's future was shaped. The four sherds of fine tableware from the late eighteenth to early nineteenth century found at the Fort Raleigh earthwork (possibly related to President Monroe's 1819 visit) may be said to usher in the era of historical awareness that still continues and that will do as long as the names of Virginia Dare and the Lost Colony remain at the cornerstone of Anglo-American history.

APPENDICES

Report appendices are archived in accessible electronic form at the First Colony Foundation's website, https://www.firstcolonyfoundation.org, and at the Fort Raleigh National Historic Site Archives:

1. Quantitative Analysis
2. Stratigraphy & Numbering
3. Artifact Distribution
4. Metallurgical Analyses
5. Critique of Previous Excavations

NOTES

Introduction

1. Sir Humphrey Gilbert's brief sojourn in Newfoundland (Norumbega) in 1583 had been planned as a permanent foothold using the patent granted to him by Queen Elizabeth in 1578.
2. Harriot, *Briefe and True Report*, 5.
3. Ibid.
4. The Virginia Company Foundation was a Jamestown-based nonprofit association of Virginia archaeologists specializing in the early colonial period.
5. Harrington, "Auxiliary Science."
6. Noël Hume, "Archaeology: Handmaiden to History."

Chapter 1

7. Quinn, "Letters Patent to Walter Raleigh, March 25, 1584," *New American World*, 267.
8. Ibid., 276; Arthur Barlowe's report of the 1584 voyage.
9. lbid., 277.
10. Ibid.
11. Ibid., 278.
12. Ibid., 279–80.

13. Ibid., 282; *Holinshed's Chronicles*, 90–91.

14. *Holinshed's Chronicles*, 90–91.

15. Aubrey, *Brief Lives*, 261.

16. Ibid., 264.

17. Quinn, "Letters Patent," 268, n. 1.

18. Ibid., 269.

19. Aubrey, *Brief Lives*, 267.

20. Ibid., 263.

21. Ibid., 265.

22. Noël Hume, *Virginia Adventure*, 102–3.

23. The 1607 Jamestown settlers numbered 104 and the Fort St. George group about 100. *Holinshed's Chronicles* (1587, vol. 3, 1401–2) stated that those left on Roanoke Island were "in all to the number of an hundred and seaven persons" and that Grenville's fleet had included a "competent number of soldiers." Cf. Quinn, *New American World*, 286–87.

24. Quinn, *Set Fair for Roanoke*, 56.

25. Quinn, *New American World*, 274; possibly written by Roger Williams, the author of *A Briefe Discourse of Warre* (1590), a treatise offering similar counsel.

26. Noël Hume, *Virginia Adventure*, 34.

27. Two surviving letters written by Ralph Lane on September 3 and 8 and addressed to Secretary of State Walsingham and to supporter Richard Hakluyt the lawyer, respectively, indicate that one of Grenville's ships, probably the *Roebuck*, remained until after the latter date.

28. *Terra Sigillata* or *Samian Ware* are terms used by archaeologists to describe a red-gloss and often mold-decorated pottery of the Roman period, most of it made in southern and central Gaul. However, in the seventeenth century, the terms had a pharmaceutical connotation. The 1671 edition of *The New World of Words; or, a General English Dictionary* defined Terra Samia as "a kind of white, stiff, and tough earth, from the isle of Samos" and Terra Sigillata as "a kind of earth much used in Physick; so called because it used to be sent from the Isle of Lemnos, sealed."

29. Quinn, *New American World*, 293.

30. Ibid., 291; Ralph Lane to Secretary of State Sir Francis Walsingham.

31. Ibid., 289; Ralph Lane to Sir Francis Walsingham on August 12, 1585. Addressed from "Porte Ferdynando, in Verginia," this letter was written after Grenville's July itinerary through the lower Pamlico Sound and up

the Pamlico and Neuse Rivers accompanied by Lane, Thomas Harriot, John White and others. On July 21, the fleet sailed north from Wococon past Hatteras Island, arriving off modern Bodie Island on the twenty-seventh. It there lay off Port Ferdinando (close by or at the now-blocked Roanoke Inlet), and it was there that Lane wrote his letter. The "Porte" prefix does not imply a safe harbor but rather an entrance or doorway.

32. Quinn, *Roanoke Voyages*, 1: 274.

33. Harriot, *Briefe and True Report*, 23.

34. Ibid., 127. Harriot's death is attributed to facial cancer, described by Aubrey as "a little red speck (exceeding small) [on the top of his nose] which grew bigger and bigger, and at last killed him."

35. Ibid., 126.

36. In the list of those who lived on Roanoke Island in the 1585–86 period, Gans is cited as "Dougham Gannes," and in at least one instance, he signed himself Joachim Gaunz. I am indebted to researcher Gary C. Grassle for access to his seminal study "German Mineral Specialists in Elizabethan England and Raleigh's Virginia," also his published paper "Joachim Gans of Prague: America's First Jewish Visitor," *Review of the Society for the History of Czechoslovak Jews* (1987): 53–90.

37. Harriot, *Briefe and True Report*, 27.

38. Accounts for the purchase and fitting out of the *Gabriel* and Michael in Quinn, *New American World*, vol. 4, 199. A bright smith was a worker in bright, polished iron or tin, rather than a heavy-duty blacksmith. One might deduce, therefore, that the purchased bellows was relatively small and more appropriate for testing than manufacturing—which certainly would have been Gans's need and intent.

39. Ibid., 200. The notion that foreigners would be impressed into cooperation by the flourishing of colorful, seal-appended letters of authority was not merely sixteenth-century Christian arrogance. In the living memory of National Geographic Society writers and photographers, their foreign travel kit included comparable "authorities" known to them as "dago dazzlers."

40. Instructions for a voyage of reconnaissance to North America in 1582 or 1583, Quinn, *New American World*, vol. 3, 242. The term *cards* meant maps or charts.

41. In volume 1 of his two-volume work *The Roanoke Voyages 1584–1590*, 51–2, Quinn, in discussing Bavin, states that he "corresponds to White as surveyor and painter." Adds Quinn, "Just, as it is evident that Harriot undertook most of the tasks indicated above [observations covered in

Harriot's *Briefe and True Report*], so did White those assigned to Bavin, except that Harriot, not White, is likely to have taken the more delicate observations by instrument, and that the two cooperated very closely on the map."

42. The original drawings now in the collection of the British Museum suffered water damage resulting from a fire in an adjoining building when the collection was to be sold at auction in the rooms of Sotheby, Wilkinson and Hodge in 1865. The cover sheet, inscribed in a contemporary hand, reads: "The pictures of sondry thinge made by S[r] Walter Raleigh knight, for the discovery of La Virginea. In the 27th yeare of the most happie reigne of our Souveraigne lady Queene Elizabeth. And in the yeare of or Lorde God. 1585." See Paul Hulton, *America 1585*, plate 1.

43. At the end of a listing of "divers other Gentlemen" is added "and John White in another shipboate," this in the anonymously authored (but probably by Arthur Barlowe) account of "the voyage made by Sir Richard Greenvile, for Sir Walter Raleigh, to Virginia, in the yeere 1585," Hakluyt, *Principal Navigations* 6: 137. Although a person of sufficient stature to be named governor in 1587, White is never mentioned by Lane, nor does he figure in the account of the expedition printed in Ralph Holinshed's *Chronicles* in 1587, which draws on information provided by Grenville that omits White from the names of the key men setting out, as well as of those who were to remain. Quinn, *New American World*, 286–87.

44. David Quinn has written that thrown overboard from the departing boats "and thus destroyed were some of the notebooks and drawings that Harriot and White had laboriously assembled" (*Set Fair for Roanoke*, 138).

45. That the collection contains other material not associated with the 1585–86 expedition provides precedent for contending that the map was drawn and painted in England and based on Harriot's original cartography. Included in the White legacy are imaginative renderings of ancient Britons and Picts whose body decoration seems to have been derived from the Algonquian ornamentation White had seen and drawn in Virginia and thus were the product of ruminations after he returned to England. Hulton, *America 1585*, pls. 65–69. Theodor de Bry would later use White's interpretations "to showe how that the Inhabitants of the great Bretannie have bin in times past as sauvage as those of Virginia." Appended to Harriot's *Briefe and True Report*, 75. It is reasonable to conclude, therefore, that this kind of reasoning was among

the subjects debated by Raleigh, Harriot, White and others after the return of Lane and his colonists in the summer of 1586.

46. On September 8, Lane wrote from the "Newe Forte in Verginia" to Secretary of State Sir Francis Walsingham accusing Grenville of intolerable high-handedness in dealing with his officers. "Sir Richard Greenfeelde Generalle, hathe demeaned him selfe, from the fyrst daye of his entry into governement at Plymmouth, untyll the daye of hys departure from hence," wrote Lane. Quinn, *Roanoke Voyages*, 21–214.

47. Hulton, *America 1585*, 174.

48. Hakluyt, *Principal Navigations* 6: 134–35.

49. White's drawing is contemporaneously captioned as follows: "The forme of a fort wch was made by Mr Ralfe Lane in a parte of St Johns Island neere Capross where we toke in salt the xxvjlh of May. 1585." See Hulton, *America 1585*, 42, pl. 4. Although the use of the pronoun in the caption can be seen as evidence of White's presence, "we" can as well be interpreted as embracing the entire Grenville expedition. It should be noted that in addition to enclosing two salt piles rather than the stated single one, the rendering includes twenty-four rather than the cited twenty salt salvagers.

50. Hakluyt, *Principal Navigations* 6: 155–56; Ralph Lane's account of events from August 17, 1585 to June 18, 1586.

51. Ibid., 6: 162.

52. Harriot, *Briefe and True Report*, 11.

53. Hakluyt, *Principal Navigations* 6: 163.

54. For an assessment of the materials Lane's people may have left behind, see 90ff.

55. Ibid., 6: 162–63.

56. Ibid., 6: 164.

57. Quinn, *Roanoke Voyages* 2: 790.

58. Ibid., note 6, where Quinn explains Diaz's wooden fort away as "the wooden building was that inside the entrenchment."

59. Ibid., 791.

60. Quinn has suggested that one of these four pieces of ordnance may have been there a century later when surveyor John Lawson visited the site and, in the fort, found "a small Quarter-deck-Gun, made of Iron Staves, and hooped with the same Metal" (Quinn, *Roanoke Voyages* 2: 791, n. 6). See Lawson, *History of North Carolina*, 61. However, the gun described by Lawson was almost certainly wrought rather than cast as were the tubes described by Diaz. For a shipboard gun of the sixteenth-

century type seen by Lawson, see Noël Hume, *Shipwreck! History from the Bermuda Reefs*, 35.

61. When building James Fort in 1607, Captain Gabriel Archer recorded that "Captaine Newport worthely of his owne accord causing his Sea men to ayde us in the best parte therof." Arber, ed., *Travels and Works of Captain John Smith* 1: liii.

62. Hakluyt, *Principal Navigations* 6: 203–4. The statement that one of the Indians was shot in the side with a "wild fire arrow" can be used to suggest that the garrison's weapons included crossbows and incendiary bolts. It is more likely, however, if the Indians had already used fire arrows to set the storehouse alight, that a defender returned an incoming arrow of a type that the Indians would immediately have recognized. There would, of course, have been no point in an embattled colonist taking the time to ignite an incendiary bolt and fire it at a noncombustible target. Harriot says the Indians were amazed by wildfire works. Thus, it had shock value to buy time.

63. Hakluyt, *Principal Navigations* 6: 201, John White's account of "The Fourth voyage made to Virginia with three ships, in the yere 1587. Wherein was transported the second Colonie."

64. David Quinn in his *Set Fair for Roanoke* suggested that White's previous familiarity with "his well-beloved island" (280) may have contributed to his willingness to tarry there. It remains this writer's conclusion, however, that White had never before seen the products of Ralph Lane's labors.

65. *Oxford English Dictionary*, compact edition, 1971.

66. Ibid.

67. Hakluyt, *Principal Navigations* 6: 200.

68. Ibid., 206.

69. Structurally, if not in plan, this description of the second settlement's defenses is reminiscent of William Strachey's 1610 description of the palisades at James Towne, cf. Quinn, *New American World*, vol. 5, 294–95.

70. See note 61.

71. William Harrison, in his *Description of England* (1587), notes that a falcon's tube weighed eight hundred pounds and measured two and a half inches "within the mouth" (236).

72. Hakluyt, *Principal Navigations* 6: 222.

73. Ibid.

74. Ibid., 223.

75. Quinn, *Roanoke Voyages* 2: 809–11.

76. Ibid., 329.

77. Sir John Smythe, *Certain Discourses* (1590), 66. Point-blank range is there given as twenty yards, noting that "out of their point and blank they do neither kill nor hurt."
78. Hakluyt, *Principal Navigations* 6: 222.
79. Ibid., 156.
80. Manteo had been twice to England, having gone first with the returning Amadas and Barlowe expedition in 1584 and again with Lane's people aboard Drake's fleet in 1586. He would return with White's colonizing company in 1587 and be made the vassal king of Dasemunkepeuc—this after he had guided White's soldiers to that enemy stronghold and caused the death of Indians male and female who turned out to be his own Croatoan people who had moved into the town after its enemy occupants had withdrawn. According to White, Manteo was "somewhat grieved" by the mistake and by the resulting casualties, but "imputed their harme to their own folly." Ibid, 205. It remains a real possibility, therefore, that in time fellow Croatoans became less forgiving.
81. Purchas, *Purchas His Pilgrimes* 4: 1728, adding a footnote of his own to John Smith's account telling how two expeditions had been sent out from James Towne in search of Raleigh's colonists but returned empty-handed and assuming that all were dead.
82. The term *chiefdom* is the appellation preferred by modern scholars and supplants the better-known *confederacy*. However, the term *chief* does not seem to have been used in a Native American context until the eighteenth century and not in the *Oxford English Dictionary* before 1814.
83. Quinn, *Roanoke Voyages* 2: 835: Depositions sent by Gonzálo Mendez de Canzo to Philip III, February 8, 1600.

Chapter 2

84. Hakluyt, *Principal Navigations* 6: 221. That White gave the date of his and Raleigh's second settlement's arrival as 1586 rather than 1587, which he uses a few lines later, is further evidence of the unreliability of his reporting.
85. Harrington, *Cittie of Ralegh*, 6–8. He noted that local residents had reported the losses extending "several hundred feet during the past half-century" but thought them exaggerations. However, local residents questioned in 1992 insisted that at least one dune line and the vale

behind it had been lost in living memory. A Fort Raleigh Shoreline Conference held at the site on December 10, 1993, brought together the leading geologists, historians and archaeologists, the principal result of which was the inconclusive conclusion that the estimates varied too widely for a median rate to be considered reliable.

86. Powell, *Paradise Preserved*, 16.

87. Lawson, *History of North Carolina*, 61.

88. Brain, "Fort St. George," 18, fig. 10.

89. Powell, *Paradise Preserved*, 23, quoting a report in the *Edenton Gazette* for April 13, 1819.

90. Ibid., 26, citing Benson J. Lossing's *Pictorial Field-Book of the Revolution* (2: 450).

91. Ibid., citing Richard G. Walser, "The Mysterious Case of George Higby Throop," *North Carolina Historical Review* 33 (January 1956): 14.

92. Holme's *Academy of Armory*, 227. Although first published in 1682, Randle Holme's work was the product of writing and research that had begun in the mid-century. The pertinent passage reads as follows: "This is a furnace for the closeing of the mouths or necks of glass bottles together…reaching above the furnice top set a strong paire of Tongs with broad ends, so that the neck of the glass being made hot, with the glowing tongs it is wringed or squeesed together, and so closely united as if it were whole."

93. That activities in the mechanical arts would be located in the vicinity of dwellings is demonstrated by the 1607 plan of Fort St. George on the Kennebec River, where a fenced area abutting the blacksmith's house contains a furnace. See Brain, "Fort St. George," 9, fig. 6.

94. Quoted at length by Powell, *Paradise Preserved*, 27–28, citing Edward C. Bruce, "Lounging in the Footsteps of the Pioneers," *Harper's New Monthly Magazine* 20 (May 1860): 733–36.

95. Ibid., 30, citing Frederic Kidder, "Roanoke Island, The Site of the First English Colony in America," *Continental Monthly* 1 (May 1862), 551. Note that Kidder mentioned but one vial, whereas Throop had indicated that more than one had been found.

96. Harrington, *Cittie of Ralegh*, 37, fig. 30. The axe is now in the collection of the University of North Carolina at Chapel Hill.

97. Ibid., note 45, quoting the *Annual Report of the American Historical Association for 1895* (1896), 58.

98. Charles F. Johnson, *The Long Roll, 1861–1863* (first published 1911), 156–57 and pl. 29. Johnson's suggestion that the small earthwork might have been erected to protect Grenville's fifteen- or eighteen-man

garrison in the summer of 1586 was not accepted by any Roanoke Voyages historian until more than a century later.

99. Powell, *Paradise Preserved*, 35, quoting R.B. Etheridge, "Fort Raleigh—Its History," *Trinity Archive* 13 (October 1899), 18–30.

100. Ibid., 79, quoting from a letter of November 26 to John S. Bassett, secretary treasurer of the Roanoke Colony Memorial Association.

101. Daniel, *Archaeology*, 172ff.

102. That Williams claimed to have dug to a depth of nine feet seems excessive. None of his cuts that have been re-excavated go as deep. Perhaps he confused feet and yards in writing his report.

103. The firepits may well have been ash-filled tree holes, many of which would be found and excavated during the 1991–93 work.

104. Powell, *Paradise Preserved*, 33ff; also quoted by Harrington, *Cittie of Ralegh*, 59.

105. According to National Park Service personnel, surprise at the reconstructed earthwork's small size continues to rank high among visitors' queries.

106. Powell, *Paradise Preserved*, 79.

107. Ibid., 37, quoting North Carolina's *News and Observer*, October 5, 1924.

108. Ibid., 212; the charter of the Roanoke Island Historical Association was signed on January 8, 1932.

109. Noël Hume, *Virginia Adventure*, 89.

Chapter 3

110. As noted earlier in this book, the archaeological investigation of post-aboriginal sites would come to be known first as "historic sites archeology"—*archeology* without the *ae* diphthong—and later as historical archaeology. The first serious attempt to define the discipline was made by Harrington in 1955 in his paper read to the American Anthropological Association titled "Archeology as an Auxiliary Science to American History." That seminal statement remains as valid today as it should have been when first heard. To keep step with scholars working in the same period in Europe and elsewhere, the second *a* was added to archaeology when the Society for Historical Archaeology was founded in Dallas, Texas, in 1967. The National Park Service accepted the name change but not the spelling.

111. Henry Forman later moved to St. Mary's City in Maryland and there wrote a valuable, though controversial, book: *Jamestown and St. Mary's, Buried Cities of Romance* (Baltimore, MD: Johns Hopkins University Press, 1938).

112. For details of the Jamestown controversy see Noël Hume, *Virginia Adventure*, 394–418.

113. Harrington was not well served by the advice of his friends and colleagues. When shown a brass finial found in the roots of a tree, this writer said he thought it came from the post of an Elizabethan bed. It turned out later that it came from a New York andiron of circa 1800 and, later still, that it had served as a prop in the 1921 film. See Harrington, *Cittie of Ralegh*, 37.

114. Harrington to Ivor Noël Hume, personal communication, May 3, 1990.

115. Harrington, "Proposed Archeological Program," 4.

116. Harrington, "Archeological Explorations," 30.

117. Ibid., 9.

118. Harrington field numbers 87 and 89, respectively.

119. Harrington field number 83.

120. Reference to artifacts being of Elizabethan style means only that they are of types that could have been in use in the sixteenth century but could equally well have seen service in the early seventeenth century. But there being no such later occupation, they can safely be associated with the Raleigh settlements. This is not necessarily true also of the metal items whose period is far less precise. In most cases, these are datable only as pre- or post-fort, that determination therefore depending on the age of the earthwork.

121. Mitchiner, *Jetons, Medalets, & Tokens*, n.p.

122. Although excellently drawn by Harrington (*Cittie of Ralegh*, 20, fig. 17), these objects have seriously deteriorated in the years since their recovery and are no longer clearly legible. Harrington field numbers 81, 89 and 99.

123. Powell, *Paradise Preserved*, 35.

124. Hakluyt, *Principal Navigations* 6: 144.

125. Harrington, *Cittie of Ralegh*, 54.

126. Ibid., 54ff.

127. Ibid., 63; entry for March 16, 1965.

128. Harrington, *Outwork at Fort Raleigh*, 14–17.

129. Ibid., 10. The ditch was recorded as Harrington's field number F65-3 and the square structure as F65-1.

130. Ibid., 34.

131. Ibid., 40

132. Quinn, *Roanoke Voyages* 2: 835.

133. Harrington, *Outwork at Fort Raleigh*, 11. The drawn plan well illustrates the relationship between fort and outwork. However, the scale should be ignored, the numbering in feet being a drafting error.

134. Ehrenhard and Athens, *Remote Sensing Investigations*, 44.

135. Ibid., 52. The brackets were AD 1280–1415, AD 235–575 and AD 360–650.

136. In 1948, Harrington estimated that the Elizabethan land surface ranged "from 10 to 13 feet above the level of normal high tide in the sound," in "Archeological Explorations," 5.

137. Ibid. 54.

138. Ibid. 58

139. Ibid., 55ff. Similar concretions, albeit of varying density, are found in Virginia's James River in developing bog iron, occasionally with wood, root or reed fragments inside them.

140. Ehrenhard and Komara, "Archeological Investigations," 24.

141. Field area MS.10.

142. These sherds, coupled with others that would be found in the vicinity of a charcoal pit encountered southwest of the fort in 1947 (Harrington, *Cittie of Ralegh*, 36) can be seen as evidence of nearby domestic occupation in the late eighteenth and early nineteenth century. Two fragmentary shoe-buckle frames found by Harrington (ibid., 37, fig. 29) are datable to the second half of the eighteenth century and may be relics either of residents or vine-snagged visitors. The most readily datable of the two fragments belongs to Merry Abbitt's Type V and occurs in Williamsburg contexts of the century's third quarter. Merry W. Abbitt, "The Eighteenth-Century Shoe Buckle," *Five Artifact Studies*, Colonial Williamsburg Occasional Papers in Archaeology 1 (1973): 44–46.

143. Fairbanks, "Spanish Ceramics," 165.

144. Ehrenhard and Komara, "Archeological Investigations," 19ff.

145. Ibid., 22. Named for Colington Island, which lies north of Roanoke Island, this Indian ware was common in the region in the sixteenth and seventeenth centuries. Tempered with crushed shell and the clay containing much sand, Colington wares differ from the contemporary Cashie wares in using shell temper.

146. Ibid., figs. 14–15. The digital processing system (GE-Image-100) was provided by the Department of Anthropology, Florida State University.

Chapter 4

147. Long known as butter pots or jars, the Fort Raleigh fragments may well have served that purpose. See the photograph on page 138. This designation for the North Devon baluster jars may parallel the established terminology for the seventeenth- and eighteenth-century Staffordshire cylindrical vessels (of Cistercian Midland Purple descent), clearly noted as butter pots in the commodity regulations of 1662. Egan, "Marks on Butterpots," 97–100; Noël Hume and Noël Hume, *Archaeology of Martin's Hundred*, 266, fig. 13, nos. 1–3; 272, fig. 15. no. 3; 273, fig. 15, no. 5, note 98.

148. When that conclusion was put to Phillip Evans, he replied that he, too, had been thinking along similar lines but associating the bricks with the mouth of a bread oven.

149. Harrington had speculated that the bricks found in the rectangular pit within his outwork structure (Featured 65-1P) might have been the bed for a forge (*Outwork at Fort Raleigh*, 14). However, he went on to dismiss that theory and to conclude that the pit was of Indian origin.

150. The assumption that the workshop debris was associated with Harriot or Gans rested on the apparent absence of any comparable research unit or scientific team left behind with Grenville's 1586 garrison or brought over by White in 1587.

151. April 12–15, 1991.

152. The grid-controlled excavation was the same as that employed at Colonial Williamsburg since 1957 and was based on what is known as the Wheeler-Kenyon system The area is divided first into fifty-foot squares and then into sixteen ten-foot squares, leaving stratigraphy-retaining balks between them. The fifty-foot square is first bisected by two three-foot balks, and the resulting quarter are then bisected by two-foot balks. The fifty-foot grid was defined on its north–south lines by capital letters and east–west by Roman numerals. Thus, for example, grid square IIIB was abutted to the east by IIB and to the north by IIC. The ten-foot squares were separately numbered in series (as excavated) recorded in the Fort Raleigh Excavation Register (F.R.E.R.), disturbed topsoil always receiving the straight number (e.g., F.R.E.R. 30), with each layer or feature below it identified by a lettered suffix (e.g., F.R.E.R. 30A). Due to the small size of many of the recovered artifacts, the applied letters preceding the number were usually restricted to F.R. (i.e., Fort Raleigh series). For details of the

Wheeler-Kenyon method of recording as used in Williamsburg, see Noël Hume, *Historical Archaeology*, 77–100.

153. Post molds are the matrices left when a post rots away or is burned out or pulled out. Any artifacts found to have dropped into the mold hole were deposited after the post ceased to exist. This is called a *terminus post quem*, a time after which the post mold was vacated. A posthole, on the other hand, was dug to seat the post, and any artifacts shoveled back into it to pack around the post provide *termini ante quem*, dates before which the post was installed. Consequently, it is of the utmost importance to keep the contents of the hole separate from the mold, for together they provide dating clues to the birth and death of the post, be it part of a fence or a building.

154. Quinn, *New American World* 5: 295; quoting William Strachey's "True Repertory."

155. The placement of test areas E.R.6 and 7 had been dictated by the discovery of a possible posthole toward the north end of the first test trench (E.R.3). With two such holes plotted, their line was projected in a southeasterly direction in the hope that more might be found to convert them into a feature of importance. Nothing convincing was found.

156. III.C.4, E.R.17D.

157. The marker has since been moved to a location much closer to the Visitor Center. Whether the ditch around it was dug as a planting bed or to aid the movers in shifting the stone has not been determined.

158. III.D.4, northern 8'00", E.R.20.

159. Not until the Phase 3 excavations in 1992 would enough of the outwork's outline be uncovered to properly understand the character of the features that the Harringtons had seen and drawn.

160. North 3'00" of III.D.3 and balk 3/7; from topsoil E.R.29.

161. III.C.9, E.R.8F.

162. E.R.8G.

163. See no. 10 in the drawing on page 146.

164. E.R.8D. This tree hole was excavated to a tapering depth of 3'11" B.M.G.

165. E.R.8E.

166. F.R.E.R. 12C. Agricola, in his *De Re Metallica*, described in detail how stibium (antimony sulphide) was used to separate silver from gold in the presence of copper. Book 10, 451.

167. III.C.5, 5/9; III.C.9.

168. Powell, *Paradise Preserved*, 34.

169. Ehrenhard and Komara, "Archeological Investigations," 24.

170. See page 139, where evidence is presented to suggest that the glass was imported from Germany.

171. Dr. Francis B. King identified the nuts as "2 fragments of carbonized shagbark hickory nutshell (*Carya ovata*) and noted that "the carbonized nutshells of shagbark hickory are very common in archaeological sites in eastern North America and the nuts were probably used historically as well" (personal communication, February 18, 1992). The finds also included an uncarbonized seed of longleaf pine (*Pinus palustris*) and part of a beetle wing. But as neither is carbonized, the possibility that they blew into the excavation cannot be ruled out.

172. Holme, *Academy of Armory*, 231.

173. Harrington's plan of his 1965 excavations (see map on page 83) did not show this three-foot balk to have remained untouched but included it in the area mapped as excavated and backfilled. Had that been so, the site's most important remaining clue would have been destroyed. As it was, the crucial surviving area (left by Harrington from both sides and Ehrenhard from above) measured no more than three feet by six.

174. Dr. Fitzhugh's response was destined to lead to a close association between the Smithsonian and the Virginia Company Foundation that proved advantageous to both the Canadian and the Carolinian projects. This relationship was highlighted by a joint conference at the Smithsonian Institution at which Frobisher and Roanoke artifacts were presented and compared. Dr. Fitzhugh went on to publish a valuable account of his team's fieldwork and related research titled *Archeology of the Frobisher Voyages* (1993).

175. A double row of small holes immediately west of the earthwork may have been footing for a camera platform erected during the 1921 filming (II.C.14, F.R.E.R. E-G and J-L). Lifelong island residents recalled many another temporary construction, among them reviewing stands erected in August 1937, when President Franklin D. Roosevelt attended celebrations commemorating the birth of Virginia Dare.

176. Those to the west would prove to be modern, but time would not permit two postholes (?) in the southwesterly trench to be uncovered.

177. Susanne Wren and Alice Snow, both wives of senior Park Service personnel. Missing from the crew this year was Phillip Evans, whose knowledge of the history of both the Raleigh settlements and the twentieth-century park had made him an invaluable resource. Additions to the Virginia Company team included Colonial Williamsburg's

onetime Martin's Hundred archaeologist John Hamant and National Geographic photographer Ira Block. Also assigned by the society was artist Richard Schlecht, who, with Ira Block, had worked on the magazine's articles on seventeenth-century Martin's Hundred.

178. The term *season* in archaeology is loosely used and embraces the time, long or short, that digging and other related fieldwork is in progress. In 1992, the Fort Raleigh season commenced on October 24 and ended on November 7, that being the time window wherein the several lead archaeologists could make themselves available.

179. The square was designated F.R.E.R. 40, and the posthole 40G. The charcoal rich area in the SW corner was 40M.

180. F.R.E.R. 40S.

181. Harrington, *Outwork at Fort Raleigh*, 11, fig. 2, feature F65-14. 1992 excavation, III.C.14, F.R.E.R. 2B.

182. Fitzhugh and Olin, *Frobisher Voyages*, 150.

183. This area included two feet of square III.C.7, balk 7/11, and the southern half of square III.C.11, and collectively numbered F.R.E.R. 33.

184. This slot (F.R.E.R. 8P) was traced in squares III.C.9 and 13, balks 9/13 and II.C.9/II.C.12 and in the southwest corner of the northern half of square II.C.12 (F.R.E.R. 49).

185. By opening another square to the southwest, an attempt was made to determine the source of the brick fragments found deep in the sandy clay in the area of the 1896 memorial, but tree roots and extensive modern disturbances were all that was found. F.R.E.R. 44 in composite grid area IV.B.13 (north 3'00"), balk IV.B.13/IV.C.1 and the south half of IV.C.1.

186. Harrington, *Cittie of Ralegh*, 36.

187. Carbon-14 dating was discovered by University of Chicago physics professor Willard F. Libby in 1959.

188. Singer et al., *History of Technology* 3: 83–85. The same method was illustrated in a Venetian woodcut of 1540. Ibid. 2: 368.

189. In addition to pine charcoal scattered in the Science Center area a small piece of externally weathered coal was found on the workshop floor (F.R.E.R. 12C). It seems likely, therefore, that the metallurgists and other furnace users brought over a supply of sea coal. Dumps of coal have been found on the Frobisher Baffin Island sites, where it presumably provided the principal furnace firing source, there being no timber fuel but driftwood (Fitzhugh and Olin, *Frobisher Voyages*, 104–8). But just as the first Frobisher voyage (1576) discovered the absence of

fuel, the first Roanoke voyage (1584) learned that wood was available in unlimited quantities. Although it is possible that a small quantity of coal was brought over for use only when high-intensity and sustained heat was required, the fragment's discovery in association with iron scales suggests that it may have inadvertently been brought with it (F.R.E.R. 12C). The geological source of the coal flake has not been determined.

190. Harriot, *Briefe and True Report*, 10.

191. Ibid., 27.

192. Fitzhugh and Olin, *Frobisher Voyages*, 143f.

193. A 7'6" x 12'00" grid-based area was opened over and around the pit comprising square IV.A.11, balks 10/11 and 7/11 and the northern 1'00" of square IV.A.7, extending west to include square IV.A.10. These areas received the following Excavation Register numbers: 42, 43, 45 and 57.

194. The possibility that the feature might be a well shaft, and time having run out in 1992, another brief "season" focused solely on the "charcoal pit" from April 27–29, 1993. The "shaft" was carried another 2'9" below the apparent pit bottom (4'0" BMG), whereupon Dr. J. Johnson, professor of geology at the College of William and Mary, visited the site and inspected the stratigraphy. Harrington had recorded the pit's horizontal measurements when first uncovered as 3'6" x 4'6" (Harrington, *Cittie of Ralegh*, 36).

195. The investigated areas were as follows: II.B.7 (incomplete), II.B.10, 11, 15, part of 16 and I.C.3; F.R.E.Rs 47, 54, 41, 51, 55 and 53, respectively.

196. Harrington, *Cittie of Ralegh*, 16, fig. 13.

197. Harrington numbered the pit 50-8. In 1992, it became II.B.10, F.R.E.R. 54C-E. His notes indicate that both rectangular pits contained comparable modern wire, etc., and were probably the products of the same operation. Harrington, Note Book No. 2, 53. entry for August 22, 1950.

198. Harrington, Note Book No. 2, 69.

199. Harrington Feature 50-18A&B and 1992 I.B.7 F.R.E.R. 47A, I.B.11, F.R.E.R. 41B, I.B.15, F.R.E.R. 51E and I.C.3, F.R.E.R. 53A.

200. Fitzhugh and Olin, *Frobisher Voyages*, 144.

201. Recovered from F.R.E.R. 41J, it is possible that this is the item recorded by Bennie Keel on October 29, 1992 for F.R.E.R. 41J as "1 small pc metal recovered in screen."

Chapter 5

202. Hakluyt, *Principal Navigations* 6: 126.
203. Quinn, *Roanoke Voyages* 2: 791. Diaz reported in 1589 that along with the artillery, Grenville had left supplies for only one year.
204. Public Record Office, CO1/5-2627, dated on the cover sheet March 1630.
205. Fitzhugh and Olin, *Frobisher Voyages*, 142, citing inventories for the third voyage (1578).
206. See 6–7 and footnote 23.
207. Hakluyt, *Principal Navigations* 6: 163, Frobisher's report.
208. Harriot, *Briefe and True Report*, 27.
209. Quinn, *New American World* 4: 197; Martin Frobisher's accounts for fitting out the ships *Gabriel* and *Michael* for their first voyage, 1576.
210. The likely alternative is that if the village site has been eroded into the sound, heavy objects of no use to the Indians went with it.
211. Powell, *Paradise Preserved*, 26 and 30.
212. Noël Hume, *Martin's Hundred*, 249–50.
213. Barbour, *Captain John Smith* 1: 265–66.
214. Noël Hume, *Virginia Adventure*, 190.
215. Hakluyt, *Principal Navigations* 6: 222.
216. Quinn, *New American World* 6: 197.
217. Sir John Mandeville traveled nowhere. His widely read and believed book was written in French circa 1366 by Johains á la Barbe, a physician of Liege who gathered his material from a multitude of sources, some valid and others spurious.
218. Lawson, *History of North Carolina*, 66. The coins may well have been Nuremberg brass jettons like those found by Harrington in the vicinity of the earthwork. It seems unlikely that money would have been left behind, although a 1563 sixpence of Elizabeth has been found at some distance from the park (see photograph on page 55). Jettons were much used as counters for mathematical calculation and are found on most early sites. See Noël Hume, *Virginia Adventure*, 39.
219. For Drs. Ehrenreich and Glumac's full metallurgical analyses, see Appendix 4; the sample with iron scale attached is from F.R.E.R. 36C, with most of the scale being found together in III.C.5, F.R.E.R. 12C.
220. Several marked examples have been found in London, most of them with merchants' symbols akin to that cloth seal from the fort. Cotter, "Mystery," 259–61.

221. For examples from silversmith and goldsmith John Coke's house site in Williamsburg, see Noël Hume, *Here Lies Virginia*, 227, fig. 86. The Bermuda series is illustrated in Noël Hume, *Shipwreck!*, 8.

222. Noël Hume, *James Geddy and Sons, Colonial Craftsmen*, 34, fig. 35.

223. Theophilus, *De Diversis Artibus*, 123.

224. Nos. 3–5 in illustration. Main cupel, F.R.E.R. 31B No. 81 and 2A (Harrington backfill); fragment of second cupel F.R.E.R.8G No. 37. For Austrian examples see Neumann, "Die Probierschälchen des Villacher Stadtmuseums," 32–33.

225. No. 6 in illustration. F.R.E.R. 40E. See Pittioni, "Zwei Weitere Probierschälchen Aus Kitzbühel, Tirol," figs. 2–4.

226. It is generally accepted that Gans was not the only Germanic mineral man accompanying the 1585 expedition. Before coming to Virginia, Gans had run tests at the Company of Mines Royal copper operation in Keswick, Cumberland—which, incidentally, was staffed mainly by men from the Tyrol. One must speculate, therefore, that the presence of Tyrolian-type crucible ware on Roanoke Island points to the presence of Tyrolian mineral men from Keswick.

227. Two virtually intact examples were found in 1959 during excavations at Henry the Eighth's palace of Nonsuch but were thought to have been discarded as late as the 1670s. One retained the remains of its osier casing. At least three specimens are in the collection of the museum at Rouen in France.

228. In an appendix to Harrington's *Outwork at Fort Raleigh* (1966), 63–65, it took me two pages to conclude that it is fair to accept the Roanoke costrel as a relic of Elizabethan occupation on Roanoke Island and to suggest that it is of French origin—which it is, though in 1995 infinitely more is known.

229. Soukup, "Das Anlaborariumlchemiste."

230. F.R.E.R. 48D, No. 22 and 16D. It is possible that the pale gray to buff color of these sherds may be no more than a firing variant in Type 2. However, unlike the rest of the flask sherd collection, these fragments exhibit multiple flecks of carbonized wood or other organic material in the clay mix.

231. An example found by the writer on the site of the Bankside Power Station in London's Southwark was contained within a wicker casing and had been discarded in the third quarter of the seventeenth century. This specimen is drawn in Noël Hume, *Archaeology in Britain*, 112, fig. 26, no. 7. A single minute sherd (max. width 4 mm.) found in the heart of

the Science Center site exhibits a sharply undercut lip and is of a fine and hard red ware. It may perhaps belong to Type 3 in the Normandy flask series (F.R.E.R. 8N).

232. Hurst et al., *Pottery Produced and Traded*, 102–4.

233. Harrington, Note Book No. 2, 105, artifact no. 103.

234. Noël Hume, *Early English Delftware from London and Virginia*, 115, fig. 19, nos. B and C (Norwich) and 5-7 (Aldgate).

235. Noël Hume, "New Clues," 71.

236. Agricola, *De Re Metallica*, book 10, 474.

237. Singer et al., *History of Technology* 3: 62. Lazerus Ercker's *Assay Book* was published in Gans's home city of Prague in 1574. The neck fragments are F.R.E.R. 31B and F.R.E.R. 40G No. 34 and the non-joining (but of comparable diameter) string rim F.R.E.R. 39B (Harrington backfill). A comparable neck fragment with a similarly treated string rim was among the chemical glassware from the Oberstockstall laboratory site in Austria that dates to the second half of the sixteenth century. The vessel is there described as a *Distillationskolben*. Soukup, "Das Alchemistenlaboratorium von Oberststockstall," 17, fig. 5, no. 9.

238. Godfrey, *Development of English Glassmaking, 1560–1640*, 247f.

239. A treatise, part of which Gans translated into English for Secretary of State Walsingham.

240. Area III.C.5, F.R.E.R. 12C.

241. Fitzhugh and Olin, *Frobisher Voyages*, 92.

242. Dr. David Phelps reports that "the Cashie ware at Fort Raleigh should not be considered direct trade between the colonists and the 'Mangoaks' (Tuscarora); rather it represents trade between the Roanoke and the Tuscarora unrelated to the English except that the latter obtained the vessels from the Roanoke." Dr. Phelps added that "the simple stamped, flat based bowl has prehistoric precedent in the Cashie series" and is paralleled by "a slightly larger (20 cm. diameter) bowl with simple stamped finish and punctate decoration from a fifteenth-century ditch at Jordan's landing, 31BR7, Bertie County, the Cashie phase type site."

243. III.C.9, F.R.E.R. 8D, nos. 7 and 19; 8F; 8G, nos. 1, 44, 45, 48; F.R.E.R. 31B and 2A (Harrington backfill).

244. Dr. Phelps reports that this "appears (so far) to be a rim treatment unique to Roanoke Island."

245. Dr. Phelps notes that the pot's temper "is very finely crushed shell which has leached out. Fineness of the shell may indicate manufacture

by one of the inland groups (Choanoke?) who used mussel shell rather than oyster."

246. Harrington, *Cittie of Ralegh*, 42, fig. 33 left, no. 89. 1992 example: F.R.E.R. 53A (11 sherds) and 55B, one non-joining fragment.

247. III.C. Balk 9/10, F.R.E.R. 31B no. 86. Bowl fragments came from III.C.9, F.R.B.R. 8E and a stem sliver from 8D no. 13.

248. Hume, *Ancient Meols*, 336.

249. Harriot, *Briefe and True Report*, 16.

250. Harrington, *Cittie of Ralegh*, 41, fig. 32, no. 98.

251. II.C.4, F.R.E.R. 10K. Although found in a layer of buff and gray sand that had the appearance of being the old (pre-fort) land surface, the presence of a wire nail in it was clear evidence of hitherto undetected disturbance.

252. III.C.9, F.R.E.R. 8D. The fishhook subsequently disintegrated while in storage at the NPS Southeastern Archaeological Center in Tallahassee, Florida.

253. All the nails were found in square III.C.9, F.R.E.R. 8D nos. 3, 4, 5, 7, 10, 12, 16 and two NN (meaning that they were not plotted in situ). The married tacks are from F.R.E.R. 31B.

254. The three sherds were found close to the root system of a large tree and were described as coming from "the bottom of the topsoil and the top of Layer A" (F.R.E.R. 57). That all three sherds date within ten or fifteen years of each other and were found less than a foot apart at the same level almost certainly is evidence of contemporary and nearby occupation. A pearlware sherd found by John Ehrenhard in 1983 is likely to have come from the same occupational source.

Chapter 6

255. Ibid., 34.

256. See note 307.

257. Harrington, *Cittie of Ralegh*, 54, and page 150 of this book.

258. There is doubt that, in the Lane-White era, Shallowbag Bay drew the three to four feet that it does today. The Moseley Survey of 1718 and 1729 shows the bay as "marsh" save for an inlet at its northern edge called Gibsons Creek. See Harrington, *Cittie of Ralegh*, 7, fig. 6.

259. An iron broadax found by a visitor at the foot of the cliff a few yards northwest of the wells very likely dates from the Lane-White period. Dr.

David Phelps of East Carolina reportedly found offshore, in the vicinity of the well, fragments of North Devon earthenware, but they have been identified more recently as coming from a Spanish oil jar.

260. A similar condition had existed in 1827 when army engineers mapped the island. See Harrington, *Cittie of Ralegh*, 7, fig. 6.

261. The 1620 Wolstenholme Towne in Martin's Hundred, though located at the riverside, was erected at a right angle to it and had a rear-protecting fort at its landward extremity.

262. Hakluyt, *Principal Navigations* 6: 222.

Chapter 7

263. Agricola, *De Re Metallica*, book 7, 223.

264. A fourth season of Virginia Company excavations carried out under the direction of Nicholas Luccketti in the fall of 1993 tested around the earthwork, reopening Harrington's 1947 and 1948 trenches and testing extensively between the earthwork and the sound in the direction of Evans's barrel wells but with no success. Nevertheless, just as Harrington's Trench P crossed the outwork without recognizing it, so anything short of total area stripping is capable of missing significant data.

SELECT BIBLIOGRAPHY

Agricola. *De Re Metallica*. Edited by Herbert Hoover. Reprint of 1950 edition. Mansfield Center, CT: Martino Fine Books, 2014.

Aubrey, John. *Brief Lives*. Edited by Richard Barber. Suffolk, England: Boydell Press, 1982.

Brain, Jeffrey P. "Fort St. George: Archaeological Investigation of the 1607–1608 Popham Colony on the Kennebec River in Maine." Ms. report. Salem, MA: Peabody Essex Museum, 1995.

Cotter, J.P. "The Mystery of the Hessian Wares' Post-Medieval Triangular Crucibles." In *Everyday and Exotic Pottery from Europe, c. 650–1900*, edited by John Hurst et al., 256–72. Oxford, England: Oxbow Books, 1992.

Daniel, Glyn. *A Hundred and Fifty Years of Archaeology*. 2nd ed. London: Duckworth, 1975.

Egan, Geoff. "Marks on Butterpots." *Everyday and Exotic Pottery from Europe c. 650–1900. Studies in Honour of John Hurst*, edited by D. Gaimster and M. Redknap, 97–100. Oxford, England: Oxbow Books, 1992.

Ehrenhard, John E., and Gregory L. Komara. "Archeological Investigations at Fort Raleigh National Historic Site, Season 2, 1983." National Park Service ms. report. Tallahassee, FL: Southeast Archeological Center, 1984.

Ehrenhard, John E., with William P. Athens. *Remote Sensing Investigations at Fort Raleigh National Historic Site, North Carolina*. National Park Service ms. report. Tallahassee, FL: Southeast Archeological Center, 1983.

Fairbanks, Charles. "Spanish Ceramics of Cultural Significance." In *Ceramics in America*, edited by Ian Quimby. Charlottesville: University of Virginia Press, 1973.

Fitzhugh, William W., and Jacqueline S. Olin, eds. *Archeology of the Frobisher Voyages*. Washington, D.C.: Smithsonian Institution Press, 1993.

Godfrey, Eleanor. *The Development of English Glassmaking, 1560–1640*. Chapel Hill, NC: University of North Carolina Press, 1975.

Grassl, Gary Carl. "Joachim Gans of Prague: America's First Jewish Visitor." *Review of the Society for the History of Czechoslovak Jews* (1987): 53–90.

———. *The Search for the First English Settlement in America: America's First Science Center*. Bloomington, IN: Author House, 2006.

Hakluyt, Richard. *The Principal Navigations, Voyages, Traffiques and Discoveries of the English Nation* [...]*&c.* 6 volumes. London: J.M. Dent & Sons, 1927.

Harrington, Jean Carl. "Archeological Explorations at Fort Raleigh National Historic Site [1947–48]." National Park Service ms. report, n.d.

———. *Archaeology and the Enigma of Fort Raleigh*. Raleigh, NC: North Carolina Department of Cultural Resources, 1984.

———. "Archeology as an Auxiliary Science to American History." *American Anthropologist* 1, no. 59 (1955): 1121–30.

———. "Jamestown Archaeology in Retrospect." In *The Scope of Historical Archaeology*, edited by David G. Orr and Daniel G. Crozier, 29–51. Philadelphia: Temple University, 1985.

———. "The Manufacture and Use of Bricks at the Raleigh Settlement on Roanoke Island." *North Carolina Historical Review* 44, no. 1 (1946): 1–17.

———. Note Books Nos. 1 & 2. Mss. in Fort Raleigh National Historic Site archives. 1947–63.

———. Note Book No. 3. Ms. in Fort Raleigh National Historic Site archives. 1940–65.

———. *An Outwork at Fort Raleigh*. Philadelphia: Eastern National Park and Monument Association, 1966.

———. "Proposed Archeological Program for Fort Raleigh National Historic Site." Richmond, VA: National Park Service ms., 1946.

———. *Search for the Cittie of Ralegh, Archeological Excavations at Fort Raleigh National Historic Site, North Carolina*. Washington, D.C.: National Park Service Archeological Research Series No. 6, 1962.

Harriot (or Hariot), Thomas. *A Briefe and True Report of the New Found Land of Virginia*. Edited by Paul Hulton. New York: Dover Publications, 1972. Reprint of the 1590 De Bry edition. Note that capitalization of the title differs from that of the 1590 edition.

Harrison, William. *The Description of England*. New York: Dover, 1990.

Holinshed, Raphael. *Holinshed's Chronicles*. Edited by Vernon F. Snow. New York: AMS, 1965.

Holme, Randle. *The Academy of Armory, or A Storehouse of Armory and Blazon* [...] *&c*. London: Roxburghe Club, 1907, reprinting the only part of Holme's monumental work ever published, that at Chester, its title page dated 1682. The complete ms. collection is housed in the British Museum as part of the Harlean Manuscripts, cf. Harl. MSS 2026–2035. Holm's first volume is inscribed in his hand, "This is my first colleccions and draughts for the Academie of Armory, Anno 1649."

Hulton, Paul. *America 1585: The Complete Drawings of John White*. London: British Museum, 1984.

Hume, Rev. A. *Ancient Meols, or Some Account of the Antiquities Found Near Dove Point on the Sea Coast of Cheshire*. London: John Russell Smith, 1863.

Hurst, John, et al. *Pottery Produced and Traded in North-West Europe 1350–1650*. Rotterdam, Netherlands: Museum Boymans-van Beuningen, 1986.

Johnson, Charles *The Long Roll, 1861–1863*. Shepherdstown, WV: Carabelle Books, 1986, originally published 1911.

Lawson, John. *Lawson's History of North Carolina*. 3rd edition. Edited by Francis Latham Harris. Richmond, VA: Garrett & Massie, 1940.

Lefler, Hugh T., and William S. Powell. *Colonial North Carolina, A History*. New York: Charles Scribner's Sons, 1973.

Mitchiner, Michael. *Jetons, Medalets, & Tokens: The Medieval Period and Nuremburg*. London: Seaby, 1988.

Neumann, Dieter. "Die Probierschalchen des Villacher Stadtmuseums." In *Annual Report of the Town Museum*, 23–37. Villach, Austria: Villach Town Museum, 1984.

Noël Hume, Ivor. "Archaeology: Handmaiden to History." *North Carolina Historical Review* 41, no. 2 (1964): 214–25.

———. *Archaeology in Britain; Observing the Past*. London: Foyle, 1953.

———. *Early English Delftware from London and Virginia*. Williamsburg, VA: Colonial Williamsburg Foundation, 1977.

———. "The Fort Raleigh Archaeological Project 1990–1992, A Prospectus." Virginia Company Foundation ms., n.d.

———. Fort Raleigh Day Books. Mss. in Virginia Company Foundation archives, 1991–93.

———. "Fort Raleigh National Historic Site, 1991 Archaeological Investigation, Phase II, Interim Report." Virginia Company Foundation ms., 1991.

———. *Here Lies Virginia*. New York: Alfred A. Knopf, 1963.

———. *James Geddy and Sons, Colonial Craftsmen*. Williamsburg VA: Colonial Williamsburg Foundation, 1970.

———. *Martin's Hundred*. New York: Alfred A. Knopf, 1982.

———. "New Clues to an Old Mystery." *National Geographic*, January 1982.

———. "Phase I Excavations at Fort Raleigh National Historic Site, Roanoke Island, North Carolina, April 12–15, 1991." Virginia Company Foundation ms., 1991.

———. "Roanoke Island: America's First Science Center." *Colonial Williamsburg Journal* (Spring 1994): 14–28.

———. *The Virginia Adventure: Roanoke to James Towne, An Archaeological and Historical Odyssey*. New York: Alfred A. Knopf, 1994.

Noël Hume, Ivor, and Audrey Noël Hume. *The Archaeology of Martin's Hundred*. Philadelphia: University of Pennsylvania Museum of Archaeology and Anthropology, 2001.

Orr, David G., and Daniel Crozier, eds. *The Scope of Historical Archaeology*. Philadelphia: Temple University Press, 1984.

Porter, Charles W., III. *Fort Raleigh, National Historic Site*. Washington, D.C.: National Park Service Historical Handbook Series No. 16, 1956.

Powell, William S. *Paradise Preserved*. Chapel Hill: University of North Carolina Press, 1965.

Purchas, Samuel. *Purchas His Pilgrimes*[…]&c. London: Henry Fetherstone, 1625.

Quinn, David Beers. *New American World: A Documentary History of North America to 1612*. Vol. 3. New York: Arno Press, 1979.

———. *The Roanoke Voyages 1584–1590*. 2 volumes. 2nd Series, no. 104. London: Hakluyt Society, 1952.

———. *Set Fair for Roanoke*. Chapel Hill: University of North Carolina Press, 1985.

Singer, Charles, et al., eds. *A History of Technology*. London: Oxford University Press, 1957.

Smythe, Sir John. *Certain Discourses*. London: Thomas Orwin, 1590.

Soukup, R. Werner. "Das Anlaborariumlchemiste von Oberstockstall, Ein Vorbericht zum Stand des Forschungsprojekts," *Gesellschaft Deutscher Chemiker* (Frankfurt am Main, Germany) no. 7 ((n.d.): 11–19.

Stick, David B. *Roanoke Island: The Beginnings of English America*. Chapel Hill: University of North Carolina Press, 1983.

Theophilus. *De Diversis Artibus*. Edited by C.R. Dodwell. London: Nelson, 1961.

Unger, Heinz Josef, and Alfred Tschulnigg. "Archäologische Untersuchungen im Saalfeldener Becken I." *Ritzenpost* (April 1990): 1–20. Saalfelden.

ABOUT THE AUTHOR

The Englishman Ivor Noël Hume was a colossus in the twentieth-century world of archaeology, internationally recognized as the leading expert in post-medieval material culture. Brought to Colonial Williamsburg in the late 1950s from London's Guildhall Museum, he imposed modern standards of excavation, recording and artifact analysis. There, an insistence on accuracy, combined with the ability to stir the public's imagination, opened doorways to the past for thousands. Noël, as he was known to his friends, trained the next generation of historical archaeologists and set an example for those unfortunate enough not to have been associated with him. His broader audience was unlimited: a lifetime production of nineteen books, twenty-one articles on archaeology (in the United States alone), forty-nine articles on glass and ceramic artifacts, seven booklets and eighteen articles in Colonial Williamsburg publications, plus two documentary films. In 2013, *A Glorious Empire: Archaeology and the Tudor Stuart Atlantic World: Essays in Honor of Ivor Noël Hume* was published. Among his many honors was Queen Elizabeth II's award of the Order of the British Empire. Interested readers may see him reflect on his life in this interview: https://www.youtube.com/watch?v=6i3k2BKz-WA. Noël's death left his report on the Fort Raleigh excavations unfinished, but he ensured that two of his long-term associates would carry it to completion.

ABOUT THE EDITORS

B oth Eric Klingelhofer and Nicholas Luccketti are former Colonial Williamsburg archaeologists, trained by the internationally recognized expert Ivor Noël Hume. They participated in the 1991–93 National Geographic excavations at Fort Raleigh, and the late Noël Hume later asked them to complete his report for publication. Klingelhofer is emeritus professor of history at Mercer University, and Luccketti is president of the James River Institute for Archaeology. In 2003, they founded First Colony Foundation, which researches Sir Walter Raleigh's New World colonies.

Visit us at
www.historypress.com